# TRYING TO CONCENTRATE

See how the invisible roils,
hand in hand with the dawn,
and how the rope of time uncoils
among oak trees into the immensity
of the air punctured
by the snap of a blue jay
as it breaks into sight and lights on a crabapple

Your breath, sigh by sigh, quiets
and comes back to the meadow
outside your window. Go right ahead:
decide, whoever you are now,
as much you as you can be,
as much you as words allow.

See how the visible roils, clouds
breaking and clustering, light
coloring the grasses, the white walls
in and out of your vision and the silence
a ringing in your ears after voices
imagined after thunder
The day is about to come into being.
You can put on your body, the morning, the river, the sunlight,
Joy you haven't believed in.

*Mary Crow, Poet*

*Since 1996, Mary Crow has served as Poet Laureate*
*of Colorado. She teaches at Colorado State University.*

# NANCY CROW

Breckling Press

QUILTING          PATTERN

orange area  CONSTRUCTIONS  #27

**Library of Congress Cataloging in Publication Data**
Crow, Nancy,
 Nancy Crow.
   p. cm.
 Includes bibliographical references and index.
 ISBN 1-933308-03-6
 1. Crow, Nancy—Themes, motives. 2. Quilts—UnitedStates—History—20th century. I. Title.
 NK9198.C76A4 2006
 746.46092—dc22                                    2005034928

"Trying to Concentrate" by Mary Crow, © Mary Crow, 2000.
Reprinted by permission of Boa Editions, Ltd.

This book was typeset in Futura, Myriad Pro, and Sabon Pro by Bartko Design, Inc.
Editorial and production direction by Anne Knudsen
Art direction, cover, and interior design by Kim Bartko
Quilt photography by J. Kevin Fitzsimons unless otherwise credited
Quilts-in-progress photography by Nancy Crow unless otherwise credited
Travel and inspiration photography by Nancy Crow unless otherwise credited

Published by Breckling Press
283 Michigan Ave., Elmhurst
IL 60126 USA

Printed and bound in China
International Standard Book Number: 1-933308-03-6

Lines should be ¼" to ½"

9/13/99

lines close
very close
than flowing
out ¼" apart

do none of this →

In terms of making my way through life,
I like to think I have an enormous reservoir
of emotional strength that helps me
make the journey all by myself. But that
is a conceit I have never had to test or
experience, because for the past 40 years
I have been surrounded by a small and
loyal band of three men—my husband
John Stitzlein and our two sons. With
heartfelt gratitude and love, I dedicate this
book to you, John, Nathaniel, and Matthew.

LEFT *Detail, notes on the quilting pattern for*
*Constructions #27, from my sketchbook,*
*September 13, 1999*

no more than 1" apart

# CONTENTS

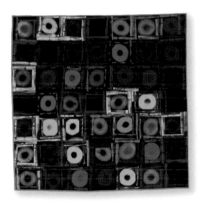

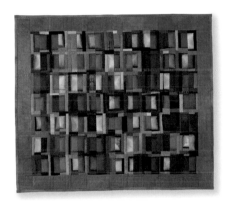

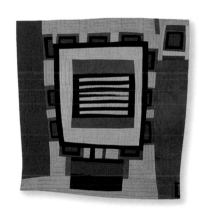

# PREFACE

I HAVE MADE MORE THAN 300 QUILTS. The purpose of my quilts is to make something beautiful but, at the same time, my quilts are a means of expression, representing my deepest feelings and my life experiences. In addition, my quilts are all about how I see color and color relationships, how I see shapes, and how I see line and linear movements. They are also about complexity, sadness, and hope.

My style of quiltmaking is contemporary, in that I want to express my experiences NOW and not copy old quilts. They are traditional only in that they are machine-pieced and hand-quilted.

I work in a 2,400-square-foot studio that is attached by an enclosed walk-through to my house on an 90-acre farm east of Columbus, Ohio. The studio represents the environment in which I want to be, in that I have large open spaces, large walls on which to work, many, many tables, high ceilings, excellent lighting that is color-corrected, a great stereo system, wood floors, enough large windows to give me a sense of the out-of-doors, wonderful storage for finished quilts, a bathroom, several different offices, and an archival storage room for photography and collected textiles.

When I work on a quilt, I put away all thoughts that are not helpful and channel my energies towards relaxing and becoming one with my fabrics. Since I work intuitively, this is absolutely important. I begin to see shapes in my head and think about how to cut them out of my huge palette of solid colors that I have hand-dyed in my basement dye studio. Never, ever do I think about what others expect or want or what will sell, but rather I look at my time in my studio as a PROCESS OF DISCOVERY. I love being inside my brain and pushing myself to think in ever more complex ways, because I know the ideas are there for the taking. It's all about being focused and disciplined, and making use of one's abilities. And about being alone, in solitude, so one can think and feel deeply, without interruption. I have definitely grown closer to myself rather than to others because I see my quiltmaking as MY EXPERIENCE, which has nothing to do with other people.

I identify who I am with my art work . . . in other words, I love the work, the experience of making each quilt. It's my life, my life's work! I feel lost not doing art, unsatisfied, anxious, bored. Everything else in comparison seems not terribly important. That is not to say I don't love my two sons or my husband. I love them dearly, but I cannot live through other human beings. Rather, I feel I can live only through using the talents I was given and, to that end, I have always had a SENSE OF TIME RUNNING OUT. I believe in just doing it and not looking for excuses because who really cares in the end? No one but oneself.

*Nancy Crow*

# Taking the Measure of Nancy Crow

NANCY CROW HAD ACHIEVED A pinnacle of success by 1990, when *Nancy Crow: Quilts and Influences*, the book that surveyed her career to that point, was published. As an activist, teacher, and curator, Crow was a catalyst and prime mover in the art quilt movement, which since the 1970s had been opening up quiltmaking from its perceived status as a marginal, tradition-bound medium into an art practice with the potential for intense experimentation and a place in the centers of art exhibition and discussion. In her own art, by 1990 Crow was a star among quiltmakers, widely admired for her technical innovations in strip piecing and for her dazzling, complex compositions, which involved inventive deconstructions and reconfigurations of historic quilt patterns melded with pattern and color relationships of Crow's own invention. With her place in art history assured and seemingly clearly defined, Crow could have chosen to devote the rest of her career to creating variations on the techniques and types of designs that had brought her fame. Instead, in the 1990s Crow reinvented herself as an artist. Today, she stands at the forefront of innovative quiltmaking and she is one of the premier colorists in contemporary American art, no matter what medium one surveys. This new book, a chronicle of Crow's work after 1988, shows her transformation.

In the 1990s, Nancy Crow went from reconfiguring historical patterns to redefining what a quilt pattern can be and how it can be constructed. The heart of her personal revolution was when she liberated her surface design and construction processes from template-controlled patterning to an improvisational approach based on free-hand cutting of shapes and unmeasured piecing. Crow's previous work required an arduous amount of analytical thought to create templates and adhere to a fixed, measured design. Today, she sees and produces patterns in new and flexible ways that permit a range of improvisatory variations within the overall parameters she sets for a particular series of quilts.

*by Jean Robertson, Ph.D., Associate Professor of Art History, Indiana University, Herron School of Art and Design (IUPUI), based on an interview conducted for Smithsonian Archives of American Art*

Detail, *Linear Study #9*. See page 154

The freedom to create a pattern without preparatory drawings and templates is like playing music by ear, without a musical score. With that freedom comes a demand for masterful skills in cutting and piecing, in order to make the shapes fit together into an integrated whole. More rare even than her practiced hand skills and more significant, Crow also possesses an unerring eye for color and proportion, with the result that her irregular shapes fit together in asymmetrical surface designs that rivet the eye with their lyrical elegance and beauty.

Quilmaking is neither a fluid medium such as paint applied to a prepared ground nor a plastic medium such as modeled or carved sculpture. Rather, quiltmaking combines two-dimensional design with constructive techniques. Pieced quiltmaking is tactile, a collage-like medium that involves the construction of an ungrounded pattern through fitting together shapes cut from fabric. (In Crow's case, she uses a rotary cutter to cut shapes that she pieces on a sewing machine.) Historically, most Anglo-American quiltmakers have worked within an overall grid structure, with shapes pieced together within each block of the grid to form a design; the quiltmaker then produces the overall large pattern by repeating the design of one block in symmetrical and mirror-imaged versions in other blocks through the use of templates.

Crow did not easily or suddenly transcend and push beyond her previous accomplishments based within this kind of rectilinear grid-and-template process. By 1990, by her own account, she was ready to abandon quiltmaking because she found the process of working with templates to create symmetrical designs tedious. She only made one quilt that year, wishing she could work asymmetrically but not knowing how to proceed. Finally, inspired by the African-American quiltmaker Anna Williams among other influences, Crow abandoned templates and began cutting shapes freehand without even a ruler, judging proportions instinctively by eye, allowing herself to cut and re-cut, throwing away shapes that were not right, and beginning to invent her own more curvilinear, irregular structures. Crow says that it took her two years to learn to use the rotary cutter smoothly, so that instinctively her hand could cut the lines and shapes her eye imagined. Likewise she had to practice and

DOUBLE MEXICAN
WEDDING RINGS

ANNA WILLIAMS

MONKEY WRENCH
BY ANNA WILLIAMS

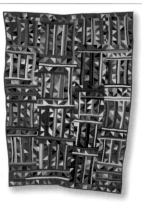

devise ways to piece shapes directly, without sketching a design on paper first and without templates. She works and reworks provisional designs by pinning strips to the wall and studying their interactions.

Along with the liberation of her cutting and piecing techniques, Crow has grown into a colorist of fabulous sophistication and refinement. At about the same time that she started to work intuitively, Crow turned away from working with commercial patterned fabrics in favor of using solid-colored fabrics that she soon began to hand-dye herself. She uses a high-quality, tight-weave Pima cotton broadcloth, which she triple dyes, creating a palette of deeply saturated and unusual hues, such as chrome orange, curry yellow, and avocado green. She further dyes batches of cloth in small gradations within each hue, enabling her to achieve delicate optical effects. Always working with asymmetrical abstract patterning, Crow puts shapes inside shapes or lines running against lines, selecting colors and values whose interactions and syncopated collision inevitably complicate the relationships of the shapes. (Perhaps an early influence was finally surfacing: when Crow was a student at Ohio State University, before she discovered quiltmaking, she studied with the legendary modernist painting teacher Hoyt Sherman, who also taught Roy Lichtenstein, another master of color and design.)

Accounts of textile history can be patronizingly sentimental, appearing to laud the domestic virtues that confinement to a home environment supposedly promotes while marginalizing quiltmaking and other textile practices as part-time crafts that take place away from the "real" art world. Nancy Crow blasts apart the assumptions of such stereotypes. She creates her quilts at home, on her farm in Baltimore, Ohio, but there is nothing sentimental or part-time about how she approaches her studio work. Crow takes herself and her aspirations as an artist dead serious, and has arranged her environment and life to maximize the resources available for her work. She has given herself copious amounts of space in which to work, including several renovated barns used as studio, storage, teaching, and office spaces, and equips her studios with color-corrected lighting, rows of tables, and plentiful pin walls. She keeps huge stockpiles of raw materials—fabrics, dyes—on hand.

STUDIO #3 RENOVATION

ARTIST'S EXCHANGE
TRIP TO CHINA

YELLOW BARN RENOVATION

A bedrock of Nancy Crow's life is her devotion to family, and her productivity as an artist is intertwined with her close-knit family life. Crow holds loving memories of her parents and gratefully acknowledges their enduring support of her creative aspirations and their profound influences as role models in forming her core values (hard work, honesty, self-reliance, loyalty). She values her siblings and lauds their achievements. Above all, she treasures her husband John Stitzlein and their sons Nathaniel and Matthew. Her husband and sons ground Crow emotionally, and they assist in practical ways by contributing time and expertise to maintaining her studios and helping as much as they can with the administrative and practical demands involved in being a sought-after artist and teacher. Although it is Crow's individual vision, energy, and daily studio work that drive her creative output, indirectly the communal and collaborative roots of quilting are echoed in the collective efforts Crow's family members make on her behalf. The most dramatic communal undertaking began in 1996 when the family purchased a 40-foot by 70-foot timber-frame barn that dated back to 1884. John, Matthew, and Nathaniel moved the barn onto their property and thoroughly rebuilt it over several years into the expansive facility that Crow utilizes as a center for teaching workshops and as her largest studio space.

One of Nancy Crow's wonderful qualities is how often she cites mentors and role models, including people she actually interacted with (her mother, artist friends) and others she has read about and admired from afar. Crow takes art making as a moral challenge, an embodiment of her convictions about how to live. In conversation, she praises as role models other artists who made space for themselves to work and persevered in their studios in the face of discouragement, neglect, competing demands, and economic struggle—many of them are women, including Lee Bontecou and Rosalie Gascoigne.

In person, Nancy Crow exudes energy, intensity, passion, and drive. She has a restless mind, her conversation moving from topic to topic in a dizzying web of associations. Her hands are rarely still, picking up a magazine to show a visitor an illustration, sorting through a pile of notebooks to find the exact wording of a quotation, pointing to a pattern made by a collection of

DYE STUDIO

CHINESE SOULS

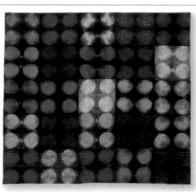

wooden fish mounted on a wall, jotting down an exhortation to herself with emphatic strokes in dark ink. She has an inexhaustible interest in all things visual, gathering information secondhand by perusing books and magazines and firsthand by adventurous traveling to distant parts of the world and by collecting arts and artifacts to bring home.

Crow ignores the hierarchical judgments of official art history and instead constantly studies and grounds herself in a history of visual culture that reaches far beyond the "high" arts of Euro-American painting and sculpture. She makes no assumptions about what sources and materials might influence her conceptually, formally, or emotionally. The collections in her studios and home supply a wide world of visual stimulation, including folk art and ethnographic items from around the world (masks, folk carvings, baskets, ceramics), an eye-popping array of textiles collected from far-flung places such as South Africa, Australia, and Brazil, and books and catalogs about both famous and obscure artists. Crow's daily environment is filled with patterning, from the rows of fruit trees on her property to the gridded ceiling of the main room of the timber-frame barn, to the arrangements of her various collections in rows on shelves and walls, to the individual surface designs and structures of her extensive collection of textiles. Piles of her dyed fabrics fill tabletops, while pinned to studio walls are illustrations from books, quotations from other artists, postcards, photographs, strips of Crow's own pieced fabrics, and all manner of found textiles with pronounced structures, such as waffle-weave hot pads and needlepoint Christmas stockings.

Nancy Crow's everyday world is jam-packed and spilling over with disparate fragments. This materially dense environment overwhelms the senses. For a different artist, the quantity and vividness of the visual information might supplant her own ideas; for Crow the immersion in an optical treasure trove stokes her imagination. Somehow she finds focus through the disciplined work of her studio, synthesizing and reducing her ideas and influences so that each finished quilt is a refined blending of disparate elements, singing at perfect pitch with lyrical beauty. In each quilt, the field is made even more tactile and powerful by dense hand-quilting. Crow is inventive in designing patterns for

BOW TIE

COLOR BLOCKS

LINEAR STUDIES

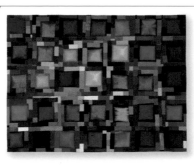

the quilting stitches that will provide a barely visible counterpoint to the structure of the piecing in each quilt. (The hand-quilter for most of the quilts in this book is Marla Hattabaugh, a master needleworker Crow met in 1987.)

Crow has worked on several different series of quilts in the period this book chronicles, all of which are beautifully illustrated and discussed by the artist in the pages that follow. *Double Mexican Wedding Rings* (1988 to 1991), *Color Blocks* (1988 to 1997), *Bow Tie* (1991 to 1995), *Chinese Souls* (1990 to 1994), *Linear Studies* (1993 to 1995), and *Constructions* (begun in 1995 and ongoing). Her last *Double Mexican Wedding Rings* quilts serve as the final emblems of Crow's earlier measured, analytical approach and use of intricately patterned fabrics. The bold graphic patterns are symmetrical and mirror-imaged, resembling the fractured yet geometrically structured patterns of colored fragments on view through the lens of a kaleidoscope. The colors are bright and clear, as if seen under a white light. The contrasts of colors, shapes, and patterns appear even more vivid because Crow frequently sets colored shapes against the extreme contrast of pure white shapes.

Crow's ten *Chinese Souls* quilts are a unique, self-contained series. They encapsulate Crow's anguished artistic response to a tragic event that she witnessed on a trip to mainland China, involving the transportation of young male prisoners to their execution.

*Bow Tie* and *Color Blocks* embody Crow's shift to a more intuitive process for making quilts and her increased sophistication about abstract color composition. In *Bow Tie*, Crow continued her dialogue with traditional quilt patterns even as she became increasingly improvisational in her approach, choosing to work with virtually no templates and cutting shapes by eye. Individual shapes grew more irregular, yet Crow still sewed them together by direct piecing with no appliqué. Crow also was experimenting with her new palette of solid colors (both saturated hues and chromatic neutrals), at first using fabrics hand-dyed by Debra Lunn or Eric Morti, then switching to hand-dyeing an extensive range of her own exquisite colors. In a 1991 interview with Penny McMorris, Crow said she was influenced by Amish quiltmakers who worked with the Bow Tie pattern. "They used values in such a way that parts of the

GUATEMALA VISIT

TIMBER-FRAME BARN
RENOVATION

Bow Tie become what I call 'floaters'." Her own color experiments included manipulating dark and light values and varying chroma intensities in order to camouflage shapes and to create her own personal versions of floaters that pulse from ground to figure within an overall pattern.

*Color Blocks* is a large, varied series that developed as Crow worked with the "one-patch" found in traditional quilts and creatively experimented with how to combine squares in larger, free-form patterns without measuring or relying on an inevitably right-angled geometry. In *Color Blocks*, Crow perfected her new color sense. Using chromatic grays and eliminating the foil of bright white, she created color structures that coalesce as flowing fields that appear bathed in colored light. She produced effective sequences of color (dark to light, warm to cool, neutral to saturated), enlivening the color patterns with offbeat rhythms, such as the single small spark of orange that accents the left section of *Color Blocks #57* (see page 125).

Crow's small series of ten *Linear Studies* breaks with the orthodoxies of traditional quilt patterns by creating structures from long linear shapes rather than square blocks. Hovering in size and proportion somewhere between an oblong shape and a line, the irregular, curving linear shapes fit together like magic to create an integrated structure without any straight lines.

Crow's largest series represented in this book is *Constructions*, totaling about 80 quilts so far and certain to continue into the future. The *Constructions* quilts comprise several subgroups, including quilts structured around parallel lines, quilts where structures are nestled inside structures, and large-scale quilts with huge, spare, beautifully cut motifs that require distance and view to take in. In *Constructions*, Crow has completely let go of standard patterning and has moved into uncharted waters in terms of profound innovations in cutting, piecing, and the design of geometric color abstractions. Regular patterns are only implied or approximated, and out-of-sync deviations embellish the basic structure. Crow is designing in a stratosphere where all the shapes, colors, patterns, and proportions that she has absorbed over decades are shimmering in her mind's eye, ready to surface and be pieced together in new, freewheeling ways.

CONSTRUCTIONS

CONSTRUCTIONS

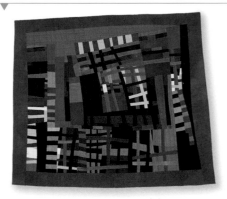

# TRANSITIONAL QUILTS
## FITS, STARTS, AND DOUBTS

**Double Mexican Wedding Rings #1**, ©1988. 72″ × 72″. 100 percent commercial cottons. Templates designed by Nancy Crow. Machine-pieced by Nancy Crow. Hand-quilted by Marie Moore with pattern marked on by Nancy Crow.

*I wanted to interpret the traditional Double Wedding Rings quilt pattern, but on a much larger scale. This quilt—like the others in the series—is six feet square.*

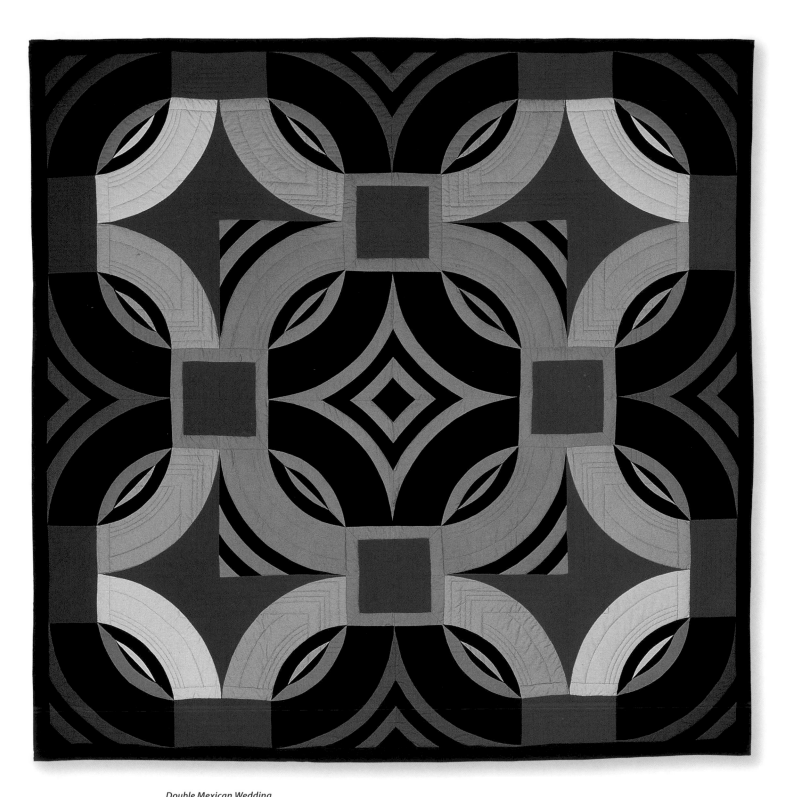

**Double Mexican Wedding Rings #2**, ©1990. 72″ × 72″. 100 percent commercial cottons. Templates designed by Nancy Crow. Machine-pieced by Nancy Crow. Hand-quilted by Marla Hattabaugh with pattern marked on by Nancy Crow.

# ARTIST'S STATEMENT

IN 1988 I BEGAN the first quilt in the *Color Blocks* series and the first quilt in *Double Mexican Wedding Rings*. These were two entirely different series. The former, which I was to develop far more intensively in future years, was based on squares and rectangles; the idea behind the latter was to blow up to exaggerated proportions the shapes of the traditional Double Wedding Rings quilt pattern. The only similarity between the two series was in the obsessive degree of visual texture and graphic impact I set out to achieve. I used a combination of commercial prints (often decorator fabrics) and strip-pieced fabrics that I had cut up and restructured. In some of these quilts, I used only strip-pieced fabrics and no prints. What I knew for sure was that I rarely wanted a single shape to remain a single shape just filled in. Rather, that shape had to be made more complex, broken up by fitting into its outline the restructured existing prints or strip-pieced fabrics I had designed and sewn specifically for that quilt.

In order for the work to be genuinely my own, I felt it had to become more and more complex. Complexity in my work ensured I was being true to myself. I did not want my work to look like that of any other artist, but because I was still working off classic quilt designs, I had to think up ways to claim individuality. COMPLEXITY seemed to be the path. So onward I ran, and, ultimately, trudged.

The process of choosing prints and making strip-pieced fabrics to incorporate into compositions absorbed me totally. I often worked for weeks, cutting strips and sewing them together, creating what I considered a "vocabulary" for any given quilt. I always made fifty percent more strip-pieced fabrics than I could ever use, because I contended—as I still believe—that I should give myself every avenue of possibility I could muster.

*Notice the fine hand-quilting by Marla Hattabaugh. I marked on the quilting pattern before giving the work to Marla for quilting.*

But . . . through 1988 and 1989 each quilt became more overwhelming as it became more complex. I grew sick of *Color Blocks* by the time I completed #3 in that series. I was not quite as tired of *Double Mexican Wedding Rings* when I completed #3 and went on to make *Double Mexican Wedding Rings* #4 and #5.

They were equally as complex as *Color Blocks #3* but in a different way. Instinctively, I knew that my grand plan of complexity as an artistic direction was not going to reap deeper and fresher ideas even as my experience grew. Rather, I was sliding into a hole. Discouragement and an increasing dislike of quilts as my medium of choice were eroding my confidence, flooding my awareness, and making me feel unsettled, unhappy.

I tried to sum up what I loved about quiltmaking and listed the following: I loved having stacks of fabrics surround me; I loved looking at, folding, and touching my fabrics; I loved pulling out and selecting fabrics for a composition; I loved colors passionately; I loved cutting out shapes; I totally—totally—loved machine-piecing. Machine-piecing calmed me, helped me to keep my chaotic thoughts and ideas straight and organized.

Knowing all this, in 1989 I began a totally different quilt that I titled *The Rat Race*. This quilt was to sum up my dilemmas. I wanted to become more efficient, more productive, more focused, and, most of all, more original. Using templates I made for this composition, I wanted to express my desire to accomplish more by getting up earlier, setting a course for the day and sticking to it, working harder and longer, and staying focused on the task at hand. But the reality was that no matter how hard I worked, I was still unsure of myself and skeptical about my goals. In this quilt my goals spin off, a muddled mess, into the air!

ABOVE Double Mexican Wedding Rings #1, *in progress, hangs on my work wall in Studio #1. In 1989, all of my work was created in Studio #1, a two-story 30 foot by 35 foot timber-frame barn dating back to the 1880s. It originally stood a distance from the house and was used for storing corn, hay, and farm equipment. I wanted a studio close enough to the west side of the house so that I could run out the kitchen door and into my work areas whenever I chose. We decided to move and renovate the barn in 1980 and hired Michael Shreyer, a fine carpenter who turned out to be as much of a perfectionist as I am. Michael worked patiently with us for stretches of time, knowing we were short of money. The renovation took almost five years. Later, our son Matthew apprenticed with Michael Shreyer. Today, Matthew is an expert carpenter, specializing in artists' studios. RIGHT While working on* The Rat Race, *I knew the goals I had determinedly set for this quilt were spinning out of control.*

*The Rat Race*, ©1989.
48″ × 90″. 100 percent
commercial cottons.
Templates designed by
Nancy Crow. Machine-
pieced by Nancy Crow.
Hand quilted by Kris Doyle.

Quilt by Anna Williams:
*Monkey Wrench*, ©1991.
67″ × 87″. 100 percent
commercial cottons.
Hand-pieced and
machine-pieced by Anna
Williams. Hand-quilted by
Marie Moore. Collection
of Nancy Crow.

I had to face up to my real dilemma . . . I needed to find a way to make quilts as ART, expressive of who I was and what I wanted to say. Frustrated and unhappy, I was ready to quit and change my medium. I seriously considered studying printmaking or painting. But no, I could not. I knew in my heart the truth—I ABSOLUTELY loved fabric and I was ABSOLUTELY a machine-piecer. Slowly, it dawned on me that rather than change direction, I needed to find a way to work more freely as a quiltmaker, without resorting to collage techniques or hand appliqué. I wanted to machine-piece freely, but I realized that the ruler and the templates I made obsessively were holding me back. I had to find a way through this wall. I looked and looked at work in other media made by outsider artists, responding to the obtuseness and originality I saw. I studied ethnic textiles, buying every book on the subject I could find. I studied indigenous architecture. And I looked anew at photographs of old utility quilts. Everything I saw influenced me, yet I still needed to know HOW TO GIVE MYSELF freedom to cut without a ruler or the use of templates.

By 1988, I had been introduced to the early work of Anna Williams of Baton Rouge, Louisiana. For the previous 30 years, Anna had worked one day a week cleaning house for Katherine Watts, a professor of Home Economics at the University of Louisiana, who owned a quilt shop. I met Katherine when she studied with me in the early 1980s when I was teaching a class at the Arrowmont School of Arts and Crafts in Gatlinburg, Tennessee. When Katherine closed down her shop, she had given Anna, who was 58 years old at the time, an assortment of cotton fabrics. Anna began to make quilts based on patterns she had learned from her grandmother. In four short years, Anna had produced enough related work to convince me to invite her to exhibit at the first Quilt/Surface Design Symposium in Columbus, Ohio, in 1990. Anna would be our first guest artist, an example of a person who had drive, focus, and the desire to express herself in her own particular way.

Since taking up quiltmaking, Anna had blazed forth, setting up a studio area in her bedroom, working nearly every day whenever there was time left over after her daily job of cleaning houses for a small number of long-time

*Anna Williams* AT RIGHT *with Katherine Watts in front of one of Anna's quilts, at the home of Watts in Baton Rouge, Louisiana, 2000.*

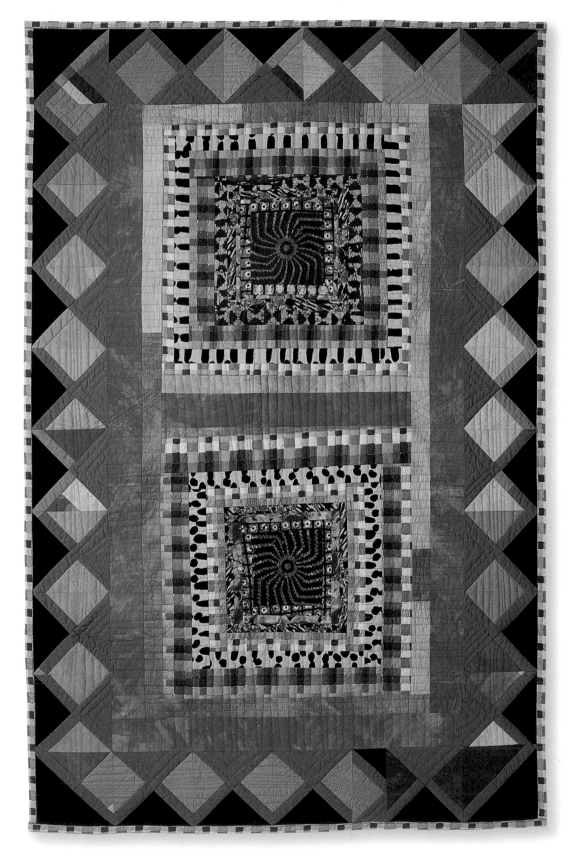

*Wax Blocks*, ©1991. 45" × 70". 100 percent commercial cottons plus hand-dyed cottons by Nancy Crow. Templates designed by Nancy Crow. Machine-pieced by Nancy Crow. Hand-quilted by Marie Moore with pattern marked on by Nancy Crow.

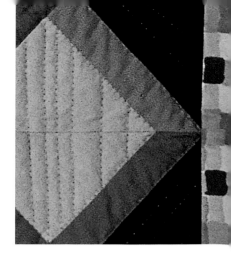

loyal customers. I was impressed, incredibly impressed. This woman did not talk about her health problems, her painful back or other complaints; she did not whine or make excuses; she did not look outward to peg her troubles to some real or imaginary event in her life or some other person. No, Anna glowed. She was focused, and she was totally ABSORBED in her work, producing quilt tops one after the other. She loved what she was doing. Each quilt I saw led to extraordinary conversations about what was important to Anna. She built her quilt tops from parts and pieces, sewing smaller shapes together, then adding more shapes to make larger units. Her crowded bedroom housed stacks of small units, stacks of medium units, stacks of large units, and stacks of finished tops. Katherine Watts saw to it that each top was beautifully hand quilted. Katherine also kept everything in order. She made records of each quilt, along with a written account of all Anna was accomplishing, year after year. Anna had her own vision and Katherine respected that. Katherine knew it was not her place to influence Anna's quilts; she was a loyal supporter, a patron who was Theo to her Vincent Van Gogh, Anna.

When we had finished hanging Anna's quilts for the symposium, I stood back and studied them. The development from the first quilt through to the last was heroic and meteoric. The energy and personality of the work shook my emotions and slapped me in the face. Anna's line edges were expressive. She played with shapes; triangles ran into one another and got cut off; rectangles and squares chased each other and combined themselves with lines. Anna didn't use a ruler or even templates. She didn't seem to care if her lines were straight or not. When I asked her about this, she laughed and said nothing. Anna used scissors to cut her edges and therefore they expressed HER WAY of making quilts. I was blown away that such strong work had been created during so short a period of time by this quiet, singular human being.

With nearly fifteen years of straight edges to fight off, I knew I had to find a way to freedom. I suddenly saw myself as a slow learner and wondered why this was so. I had always prided myself on self-awareness, but how aware was I? By 1990, I lunged into a period of fits, starts, and doubts, creating the peculiar mix of quilts showcased in this chapter as I struggled to find my way forward.

*Completed two years after* The Rat Race, Wax Blocks *was a further attempt to work more freely. Again I used templates but I began to eschew the preprinted designs of commercial fabrics. I was definitely still struggling. This was an odd-ball quilt—it related to nothing else I was working on around that time.*

*Double Mexican Wedding Rings #4*, ©1988–1990. 72" × 72". 100 percent commercial cottons. Templates designed by Nancy Crow. Machine-pieced by Nancy Crow. Hand-quilted by Marie Moore with pattern marked on by Nancy Crow.

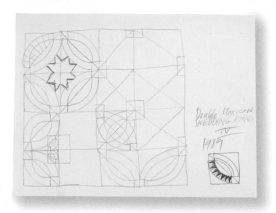

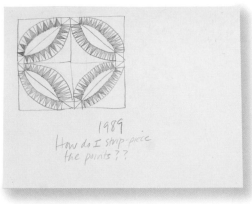

TOP *Sketches for* Double Mexican Wedding Rings # 4 *from 1989.* ABOVE Double Mexican Wedding Rings #4 *as a work-in-progress in September 1988. This was a very complex quilt in terms of all the strip-pieced fabrics I spent weeks making before I started; most of these fabrics were then further cut-up to be restructured in small units. I really loved this piece!*

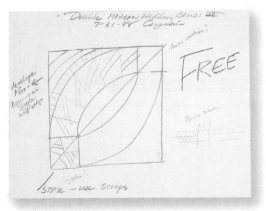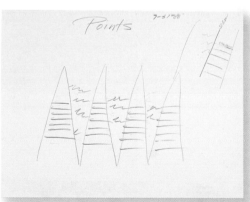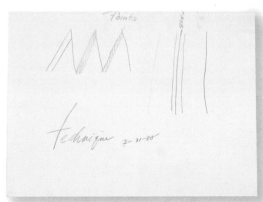

TOP *My work wall, set up with "items to think about" before starting on* Double Mexican Wedding Rings #4 *in April 1988.* ABOVE *Sketches for* Double Mexican Wedding Rings #4 *from 1988.*

1

2

3

4

5

6

7

8

# CONSTRUCTING STUDIO #3 FROM A 1880s GRANARY BARN

LIFE EXPERIENCES AND EVENTS have always influenced my work as an artist. When I look back on the quilts I made during this period of fits, starts, and doubts in the late 1980s and early 1990s, I find the work to be inseparable from the farm renovations that were going on around me. While my quilts evolved, I was working in Studio #1, an 1880s barn that we had relocated on our farm and which eventually became an extension to our Federal-style house. Early in 1990, new owners of a neighboring property gave us another barn structure they felt they would never use. Also built around 1880, it had served as a small granary, measuring about 16 feet by 20 feet. Upon examining it, we decided we could haul the barn over to our farm ourselves and attach it to the west side of Studio #1. It would be transformed into a small room for keeping archival photography and for storing my quilts.

Since the barn was in excellent condition, considering its age, our carpenter Michael Shreyer decided to encase the entire structure with extra-thick insulation, then with new vertical siding. Next, he built new plaster walls inside, right on top of the existing wood walls. Because the walls are very thick, Studio #3 stays quite temperate throughout all seasons.

Since it is small and soundproof, I find Studio #3 to be the perfect place to work when I need absolute quiet. Outside the two windows, our orchard flanks the south and west corner of the structure. If I open the windows, I can watch birds and listen to the rustle of branches and leaves. It is an ideal spot to daydream. (All photos are ©1990 to 1993 by Nancy Crow, except as noted.)

FROM TOP LEFT, PHOTO 1 *My sons Nathaniel (left) and Matthew jack up the small granary barn on our neighbor's farm in preparation for sliding it onto a small flatbed wagon.* PHOTO 2 *My husband John Stitzlein on our old tractor, pulling the granary up our lane.* PHOTO 3 *John pulls the granary as close as he can to the west side of Studio #1.* PHOTO 4 *The renovation began in 1991. Michael Shreyer was chief carpenter and was helped by the three Stitzlein men. We had to wait a full year before we had saved enough money for the project.* PHOTO 5 *A short corridor was built to attach the two studios.* PHOTO 6 *Seen here from the back (north side), complete with exit door, the renovation was completed in Spring 1993.*

9

10

11

PHOTO 7 *Standing in front of my 2,400-square-foot studio, a renovated 1880s barn, with Studio #2 addition (added in 1987–1988). In all, attached to my house are three studios, Studio #1, Studio #2, and Studio #3.* PHOTO 8 *Studio interior during the renovation, looking west into the open room.* PHOTO 9 *Wood cabinets, made of solid tulip poplar, provide storage along the south wall of Studio #3 for all photography and other archival materials.* PHOTO 10 *Behind the sliding barn doors on the north wall of Studio #3 are shelves used to store quilts and deep drawers to hold textiles.* PHOTO 11 *This photograph was taken in January 1994, looking into Studio #3 as I was working on the catalog for my 1995 show at the Smithsonian's Renwick Gallery. On the west wall is an antique silk quilt.*

TOP Double Mexican Wedding Rings #5 *was fabulously and densely hand-quilted by Kris Doyle, who chose to wind in and around all the minute patterns.* ABOVE LEFT AND CENTER *The quilt under construction in February 1990. I titled this quilt* Double Afro-American Weddings Rings, *but then reverted to* Double Mexican Wedding Rings #5. *Somehow, I thought the term* Afro-American *would allow me some sort of freedom. In a way, it did—I found I was able to work more freely by piecing odd shapes onto a background fabric, rather than relying on templates for the entire quilt.* ABOVE RIGHT *The finished quilt is pinned to a barn for photography in the days before I hired a professional photographer to shoot inside my studio.*

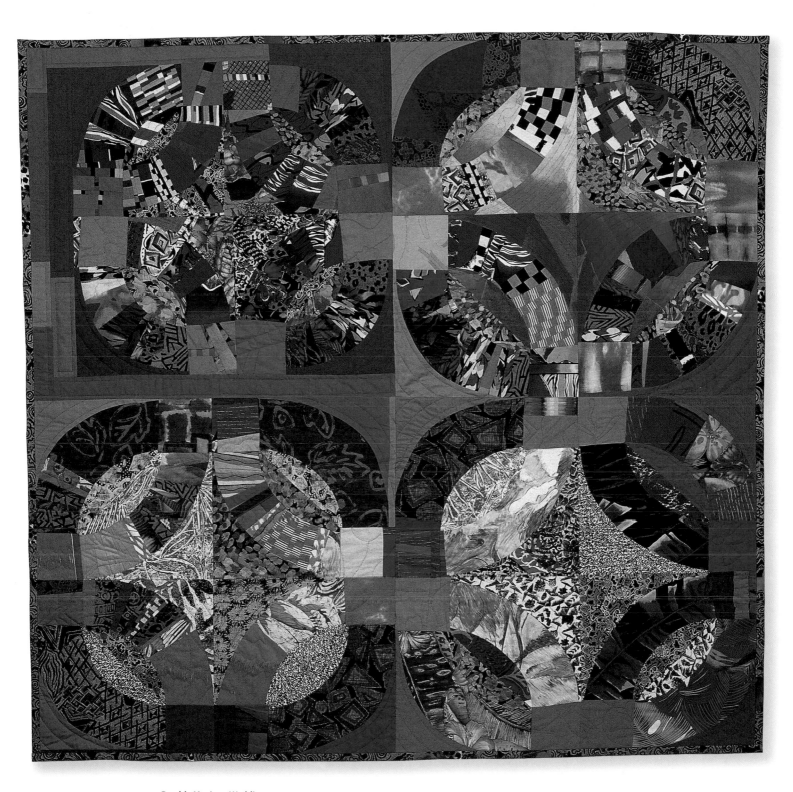

**Double Mexican Wedding
Rings #5**, ©1990. 72″ × 72″.
100 percent commercial
and hand-dyed cottons.
Templates designed by
Nancy Crow. Machine-
pieced by Nancy Crow.
Hand-quilted by Kris Doyle.

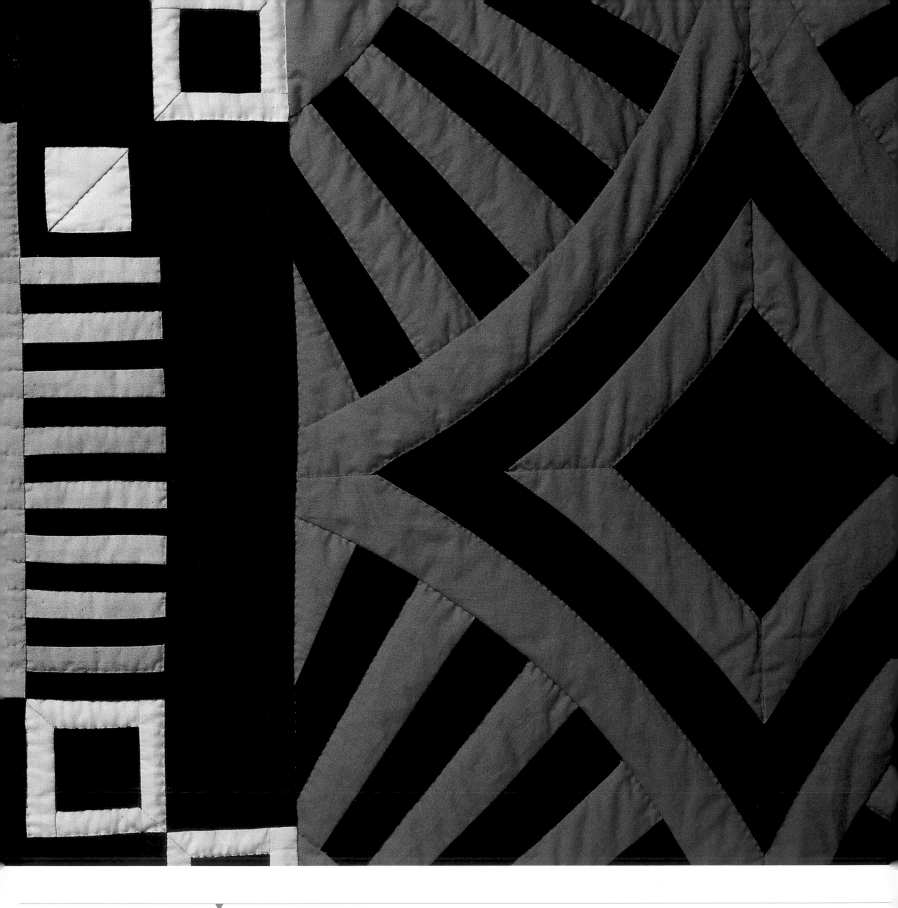

*I struggled with this quilt because by this time I knew I was going backward instead of developing. Yet I felt so familiar with the shapes used in all the quilts in this series that I could not let go of them. As a result, my work became very uptight, which is exactly what happens every time I am in a death struggle with a composition. Everything I had tried to accomplish in Double Mexican Wedding Rings #5 seemed lost as I worked on this blue version of the design. On the positive side, I did create very, very fine strip-piecing, perfectly engineered for this quilt. I spent my time being in love with perfect engineering—then I called it quits forever with Double Mexican Wedding Rings.*

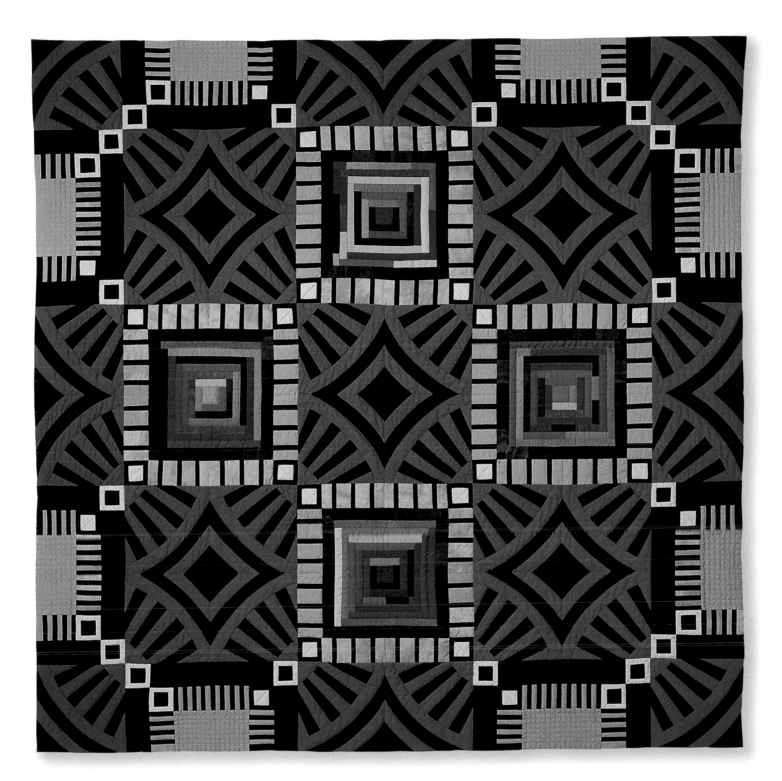

*Double Mexican Wedding Rings #6*, ©1991–1992. 72″ × 72″. 100 percent commercial cottons. Templates designed by Nancy Crow. Machine-pieced by Nancy Crow. Hand-quilted by Marie Moore with pattern marked on by Nancy Crow.

LEFT Double Mexican Wedding Rings #6 *under construction in January 1991.* TOP *The quilt occupied my work table for months on end, yet still I felt I wasn't moving forward.* ABOVE *It was still under construction more than six months later, in August 1991.*

*Study #1* ©1991.
Approximately 40" × 40".
100 percent commercial
cottons plus hand-dyed
cottons by Nancy Crow.
Machine-pieced by
Nancy Crow. Hand-
quilted by Kris Doyle
with pattern denoted by
Nancy Crow. Photograph
by Nancy Crow.

***Study #2*** ©1991.
Approximately 40" × 40".
100 percent commercial
cottons plus hand-dyed
cottons by Nancy Crow.
Machine-pieced by
Nancy Crow. Hand-
quilted by Kris Doyle
with pattern denoted by
Nancy Crow. Photograph
by Nancy Crow.

Study #1 *and* Study #2 *were attempts at working more freely. I sold both quilts immediately after*
*making them and kept no record of who bought them. Other than these slides that I shot myself,*
*I have no professional photographs of them. As I study them today, I realize they were a precursor*
*to later work I created in the* Color Blocks *series during 1994 and 1995 (see pages 117–135).*

# COLOR BLOCKS I

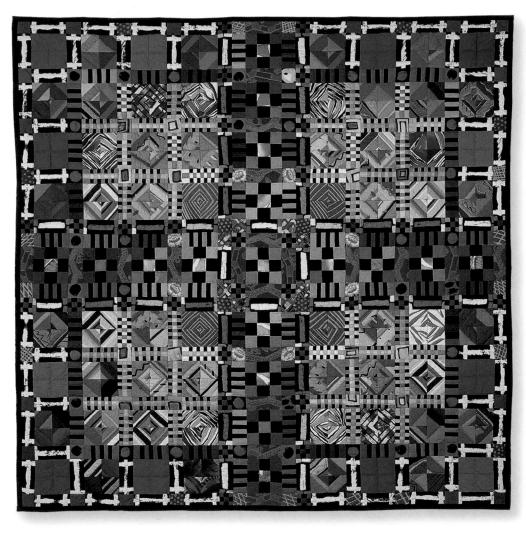

*Color Blocks #1*, ©1988. 62″ × 62″. 100 percent commercial cotton prints. Machine-pieced by Nancy Crow. Hand-quilted by Elizabeth Miller with pattern denoted by Nancy Crow.

*I considered visual complexity to be "my voice" during the period when I made the early Color Blocks quilts. I achieved complex results by my own particular methods of restructuring strip-pieced fabrics that I made, and then combining them with commercial prints. These three quilts were part of my voice, which was about to change.*

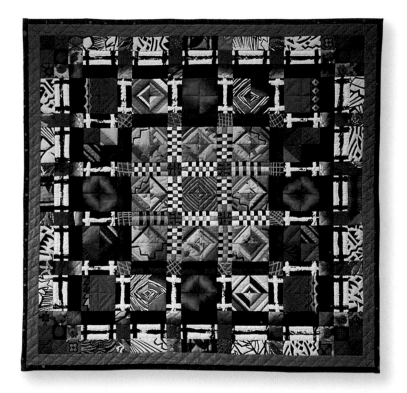

*Color Blocks #2*, ©1988. 44″ × 44″. 100 percent commercial cotton prints. Machine-pieced by Nancy Crow. Hand-quilted by Elizabeth Miller with pattern denoted by Nancy Crow. Photograph by Nancy Crow.

*Color Blocks #3*, ©1989. 72″ × 71″. 100 percent commercial cotton prints. Machine-pieced by Nancy Crow. Hand-quilted by Marie Moore with pattern denoted by Nancy Crow.

# ARTIST'S STATEMENT

COLOR BLOCKS #1, COLOR BLOCKS #2, AND *Color Blocks #3* (1988 to 1989) all belong to the culmination of a period of visual complexity that I explored throughout the 1980s. I considered visual complexity to be "my voice" during those years and achieved complex results by my own particular methods of restructuring strip-pieced fabrics that I made, and then combining them with commercial prints. These three quilts were part of my voice, which was about to change.

By 1990 I decided to return to the *Color Blocks* series and start anew with *Color Blocks #4*. I made the following important decisions, which were to investigate only the square as "motif"; to drop commercial prints, to start relying on solids, and to continue the series by exploring simplicity. I hoped I would be able to make a breakthrough to some sort of needed freedom.

Since I had always loved squares and I wanted something that seemed familiar with which to start again, I decided to use one-patch, four-patch, and nine-patch formats. As I thought about how to "fill" those formats, I began strip-piecing solids, both commercial and hand-dyed. At that time I was buying hand-dyed cottons from others and had accumulated a stash of beautiful solids hand-dyed by Eric Morti. I included those alongside the large numbers of commercial solids that were already part of my inventory. I spent weeks strip-piecing simple graphic combinations of colors that I cut up to look like strings of smaller squares. Using these, I finished *Color Blocks #4*, knowing full well that it did not have the presence of *Color Blocks #1*. But I was happy to be working, and the quilt was a starting point for finding a new way into my work.

LEFT Color Blocks #3 *under construction in Studio #1 in March 1989.* ABOVE *A detail from* Color Blocks #4.

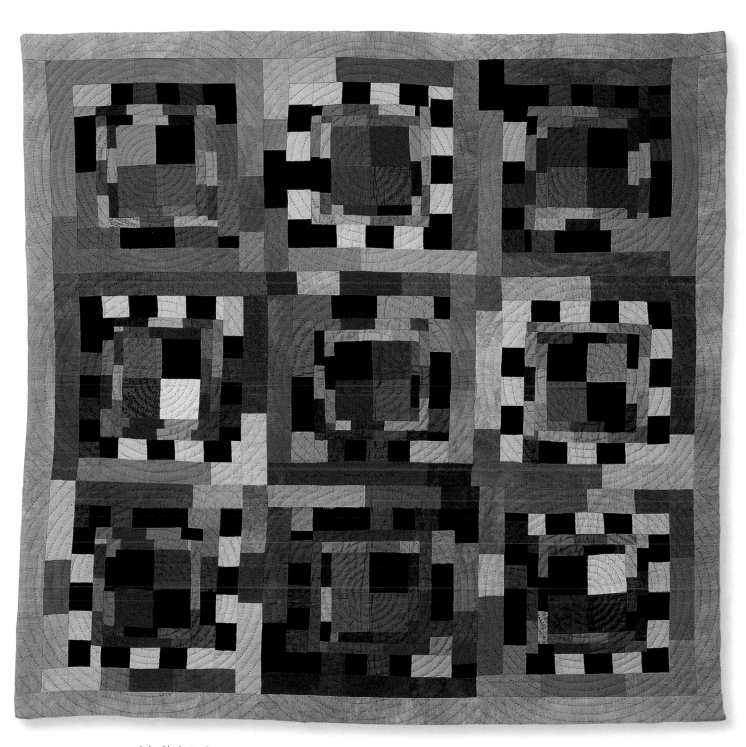

*Color Blocks #4*, ©1990.
29½" × 29". 100 percent
cotton fabric hand-dyed
by Eric Morti. Machine-
pieced by Nancy Crow.
Hand-quilted by Kris Doyle
with pattern denoted by
Nancy Crow.

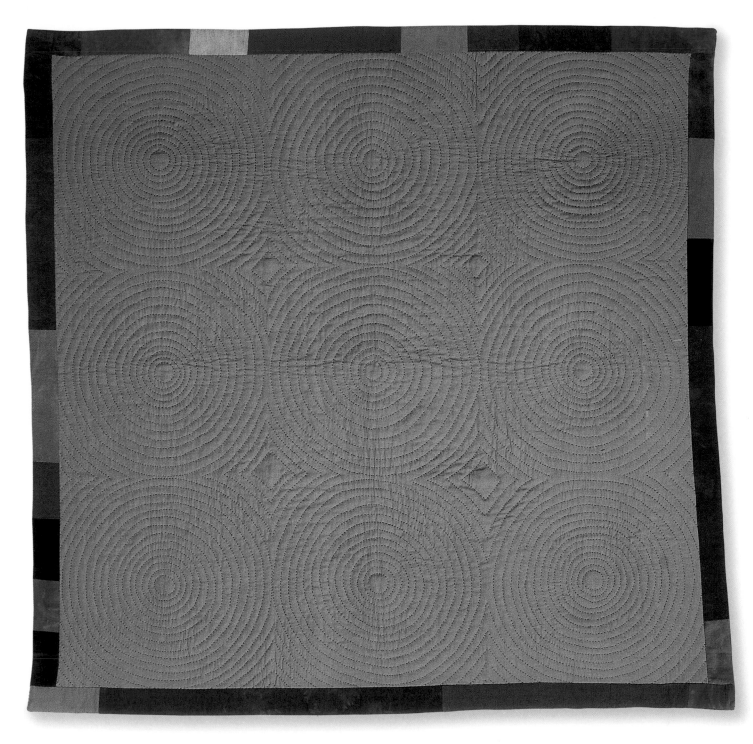

*Color Blocks #4*, back view.

During this same time period, I also began accumulating a stash of large geometric prints composed of parallel lines and shapes, such as squares and circles, that had been resist-dyed by Debra Lunn. I used some of these in *Color Blocks #5*, a one-patch made up of 20 squares that I chose to keep very simple with the use of a four-inch template. This quilt became a compositional study for larger works made during 1992 and 1993, in particular, *Color Blocks #24*, *Color Blocks #31*, *Color Blocks #38*, *Color Blocks #39*, and *Color Blocks #40* (see pages 99, 110, 114, and 115).

*Color Blocks #6* to *Color Blocks #14* tumbled out, one after the other, in 1991, as I played with random placements of colors and sizes using a one-patch or a four-patch format, or a combination of the two. I used only commercial solids plus my strip-pieced fabrics and very small templates. While working on the quilts I felt unhindered but aware that these small intimate pieces were only the beginning of a journey I had started.

With *Color Blocks #15*, I began differently. I first pulled a fresh palette of only my own hand-dyed solids (see pages 46 and 47). Changing palettes excited me and pushed me to be more playful. I cut strips from these solids and sewed them around Lunn's resist-dyed squares. Although I was still using a ruler, I did not use any templates. For the first time, I allowed the squares to become many different sizes, which caused a problem in the end because I had to figure out how I could put them together into a final composition. This became an engineering challenge—a puzzle to be figured out. BINGO. I discovered I LOVED engineering! I had stumbled into the beginnings of a way to work without templates. I studied this quilt and grasped that I was on my way to freedom!

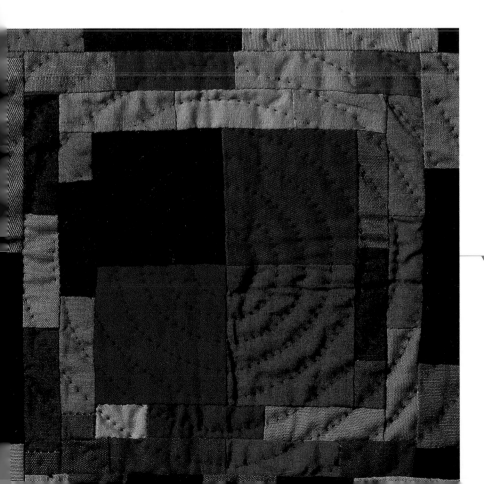

For Color Blocks #4, I spent weeks strip-piecing simple combinations of color together that I then cut up so that they looked like strings made up of smaller squares.

# MOVING AND REBUILDING
# THE YELLOW BARN

IN 1989, WHEN OUR SONS were eighteen and nineteen years old, my husband decided it was time for them to learn how to dismantle and then put back together a post-and-beam timber-frame barn. (John had also decided that he needed a better workshop and studio for himself.) After spending months looking for a barn to buy and relocate, he found one that suited him and paid the owners $600 for it. The barn stood four miles away from our farm on the Poff family homestead. It had been built around 1884, constructed out of chestnut and American beech. When I look at the composition of the barn's timbers in these photographs, I recognize the impact of the barn reconstruction on my work . (All photographs  except photograph #1, an early undated photograph, are ©1989 to 1996 by Nancy Crow.)

FROM TOP RIGHT, PHOTO 1 *The barn, in its original location, four miles away from our farm.* PHOTO 2 *The barn was finished, painted yellow, and the cupolas decorated in time for Christmas 1996. We call it the Yellow Barn.* PHOTO 3 *Dismantling the original structure in October 1989.* PHOTO 4 *To remove the original slate, John tied himself to the peak of the roof and slid the slates down to Matthew at the top of the ladder, who sent them down a shute to Nathaniel. As careful as they were, half of the the slates broke.* PHOTO 5 *Though there was an attempt to save the original cupolas, all three were so rotted out that they fell to the ground.* PHOTO 6 *A group of Ohio Amish carpenters dismantling the posts and beams.*

PHOTOS 7 TO 9 *The Amish carpenters beginning the process of re-erecting the timbers at our farm. They used a crane to hoist the timbers while connecting the beams with pegs.* PHOTO 10 *Looking up through the timbers after the structure was pegged back together.* PHOTO 11 *The original boards put back in place, serendipitously.* PHOTO 12 *Pushing and pulling the heavy roof of one of the new cupolas up a hay shute.* PHOTO 13 *Matthew and Nathaniel lifting the roof onto the side walls of one of the cupolas. After taking careful measurements, Matthew masterminded the building of the cupolas (except for the standing-seam roofs) using the original chestnut boards.* PHOTOS 14 AND 15 *The south side of the barn showing the windows before and after they were dressed out in tramp-art inspired trim.*

*Color Blocks #5*, ©1991. 18″ × 18″. 100 percent cotton fabric resist-dyed by Lunn Fabrics. Fabrics cut and machine-pieced by Nancy Crow. Hand-quilted by Kris Doyle with pattern denoted by Nancy Crow.

Color Blocks #5 *relates to later works in the series,* Color Blocks #24, Color Blocks #31, *and* Color Blocks #38 *through* Color Blocks #40 (see pages 99, 110, and 114–115). RIGHT *Ideas and a sketch for the series, February 1991.*

February 20, 1991

Since my brain wants to course off in
any direction it wants to, I just might as
well draw up my currents thots/ideas
that you will see now come (after) what is
on these pages, just 6 pages away!

# BLOCKS (Single ONE PATCH)

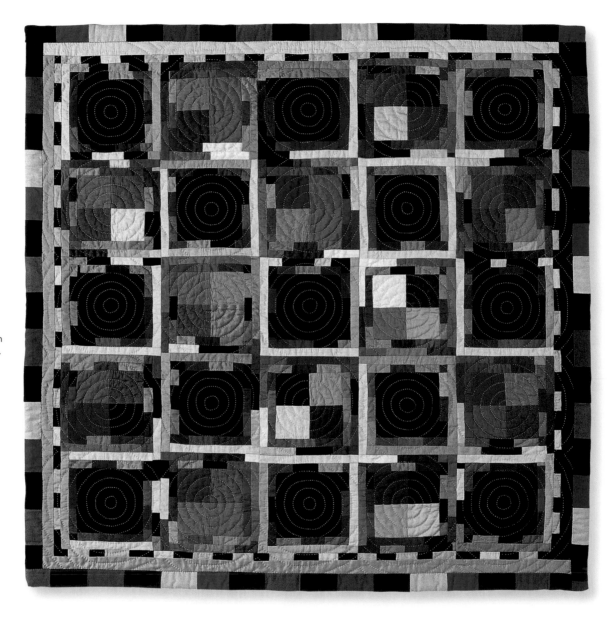

*Color Blocks #6*, ©1991. 34″ × 34″. 100 percent cotton fabric. Fabrics cut into and machine-pieced by Nancy Crow. Hand-quilted by Marla Hattabaugh with pattern denoted by Nancy Crow.

*Color Blocks #15*, ©1991.
32½″ × 33″. 100 percent
cotton fabrics hand-
dyed by Eric Morti and
Nancy Crow. Resist-dyed
cottons by Lunn Fabrics.
Fabrics cut into directly
and machine-pieced by
Nancy Crow. Hand-quilted
by Marla Hattabaugh
with pattern denoted by
Nancy Crow.

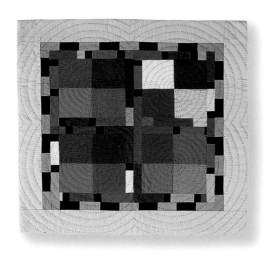

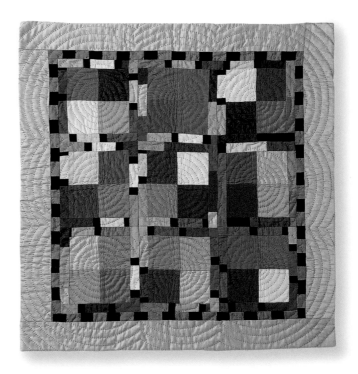

**Color Blocks #9**, ©1991.
14″ × 13½″. 100 percent
cotton fabrics. Fabrics
cut and machine-pieced
by Nancy Crow. Hand-
quilted by Kris Doyle
with pattern denoted by
Nancy Crow. Photograph
by Nancy Crow.

**Color Blocks #10**, ©1991.
19″ × 19″. 100 percent
cotton fabrics. Fabrics cut
and machine-pieced by
Nancy Crow. Hand-quilted
by Kris Doyle with pattern
denoted by Nancy Crow.

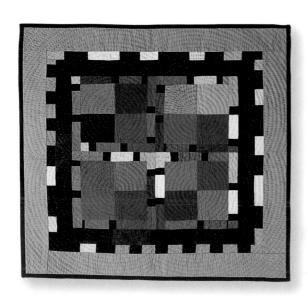

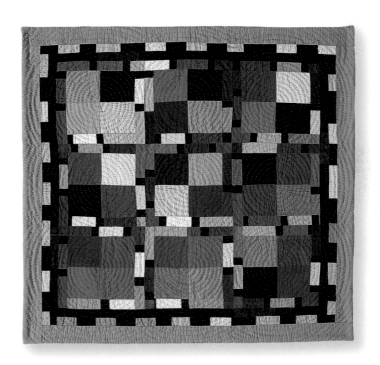

**Color Blocks #13**, ©1991.
16½″ × 16″. 100 percent
cotton fabrics. Fabrics
cut and machine-pieced
by Nancy Crow. Hand-
quilted by Brenda Stultz
with pattern denoted by
Nancy Crow. Photograph
by Nancy Crow.

**Color Blocks #14**, ©1991.
19½″ × 18½″. 100 percent
cotton fabrics. Fabrics
cut and machine-pieced
by Nancy Crow. Hand-
quilted by Brenda Stultz
with pattern denoted by
Nancy Crow.

**Color Blocks #7**, ©1991.
12½″ × 13½″. 100 percent
cotton fabrics. Fabrics
cut into and machine-
pieced by Nancy Crow.
Hand-quilted by Marla
Hattabaugh with pattern
denoted by Nancy Crow.
Photograph by
Nancy Crow.

**Color Blocks #8**, ©1991.
20½″ × 20½″. 100 percent
cotton fabric. Fabrics cut
and machine-pieced by
Nancy Crow. Hand-quilted
by Marla Hattabaugh
with pattern denoted by
Nancy Crow. Photograph
by Nancy Crow.

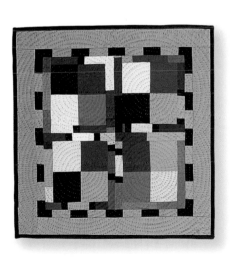

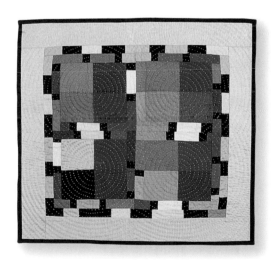

**Color Blocks #11**, ©1991.
13½″ × 14″. 100 percent
cotton fabrics. Fabrics
cut and machine-pieced
by Nancy Crow. Hand-
quilted by Brenda Stultz
with pattern denoted by
Nancy Crow. Photograph
by Nancy Crow.

**Color Blocks #12**, ©1991–1992.
14½″ × 14″. 100 percent
cotton fabrics. Fabrics cut
and machine-pieced by
Nancy Crow. Hand-quilted
by Brenda Stultz with pattern
denoted by Nancy Crow.
Photograph by Nancy Crow.

1

2

3

4

5

# DYE STUDIO

AFTER I FINISHED *Color Blocks #14*, I decided I had to start dyeing my own colors, my own palette. Although I wanted to use only supersaturated solids, I could not find any to buy. So I set up a makeshift dye studio in the basement under Studio #1. The space was awkward and had no sink, forcing me to use garden hoses and five-gallon buckets. As summer approached, I moved out into the driveway to work in the sun, where the heat helped produce incredible results. I was hooked— I couldn't stop dyeing! Piles of finished fabrics took over my studio tables until I began stacking them on the floor around the tables. I decided the time had come to do a total makeover of the basement; I wanted an efficient, well-designed space for my dyeing activities. Once again I enlisted Mike Shreyer, my long-time carpenter, to start the renovation. (All photographs are ©1992 to 1994 by Nancy Crow except as noted.)

6

7

©1995 BY J. KEVIN FITZSIMONS

8

9

FROM TOP LEFT, PHOTO 1 *Stairs leading down into the basement under Studio #1, where I did most of my hand-dyeing before setting up the dye studio.* PHOTO 2 *At center back is the wringer/washer I used when dyeing to help wring out excess dye and water. To the left are the regular washer and dryer I used to process the dyed fabrics, vented out the window.* PHOTO 3 *I still use five-gallon buckets like the ones lined up here. I can dye ten two-yard cuts or a total of 20 yards at a time in each bucket.* PHOTO 4 *Dyeing out in the driveway in front of our house in August 1993.*

©1995 BY J. KEVIN FITZSIMONS

©1995 J. KEVIN FITZSIMONS  10

11

PHOTO 5 *Michael Shreyer building low shelving for under the dye tables. These shelves now hold prepared-for-dyeing (PFD) fabrics that come on 100-yard rolls.* PHOTO 6 *Shelving above the stainless steel commercial three-bay sink provides storage for containers and other items.* PHOTO 7 *Rolls of 100-yard white PFD fabrics waiting to be dyed.* PHOTO 8 *Dyeing using squirt bottles filled with liquid dye.* PHOTO 9 *Jars of Procion MX powder dyes and rolls of fabrics in the newly renovated dye studio.* PHOTO 10 *Interior view of Studio #1 with hand-dyed fabrics.* PHOTO 11 *Strips of hand-dyed fabrics pinned to the wall.*

# BOW TIE
## MOVING FORWARD

*Bow Tie #1*, ©1991.
47½" × 44½". 100 percent
cotton fabric hand-dyed
by Fric Morti. Machine-
pieced by Nancy Crow.
Hand-quilted by Kris Doyle
with pattern denoted by
Nancy Crow.

*In Bow Tie #1, I incorporated strip-piecing but let go
of this technique in later quilts in this series.*

**Bow Tie #2**, ©1991.
35½″ × 35½″. 100 percent
cotton fabric hand-dyed
by Eric Morti and Nancy
Crow. Machine-pieced by
Nancy Crow. Hand-quilted
by Marla Hattabaugh
with pattern denoted by
Nancy Crow.

*I started* Bow Tie #2 *and* Bow Tie #3 *in 1991. Each breakthrough in my thinking signified a loosening up of control, as I gave myself permission to be free, to let things happen more naturally. By the time I started making these quilts, I had a growing stack of gorgeous hand-dyed colors, some by Eric Morti and the rest by me. I was eager to use them so I decided to work on pure shapes using only solid colors/values.*

# ARTIST'S STATEMENT

SPARENESS HAS ALWAYS ATTRACTED ME, the spareness of shape to shape. In particular, I am deeply interested in how shapes might be controlled by value shifts and how this may lead to more abstract compositions. In early 1991, my desire to explore asymmetrical freedom led me to study the paintings of abstract expressionists produced during the 1940s to the 1970s. I then went back, over and over, through all my books of antique quilts, picking out those

*Bow Tie #3*, ©1991. 35½" × 35½". 100 percent cotton fabric hand-dyed by Eric Morti and Nancy Crow. Machine-pieced by Nancy Crow. Hand-quilted by Marla Hattabaugh with pattern denoted by Nancy Crow.

*Bow Tie #4*, ©1991. 22″ × 21″. 100 percent cotton fabric hand-dyed by Eric Morti with resist-dyeing by Lunn Fabrics. Fabrics cut into directly and machine-pieced by Nancy Crow. Hand-quilted by Kris Doyle with pattern denoted by Nancy Crow.

that had been composed of classical patterns but changed into oftentimes startling original compositions by sweet imagination, serendipity, and the utterly fresh use of color and value.

For some reason (possibly its simplicity), the traditional Bow Tie quilt pattern intrigued me. I found early Amish and non-Amish versions of the pattern that blew me away. The compositions were dynamite! I knew instinctively that if I wanted to concentrate on figure/ground relationships in a more abstract way, I needed to start out with simple shapes and a simple format. The classic Bow Tie design seemed to be the answer.

*Bow Tie #5*, ©1991.
23″ × 23″. 100 percent
cotton fabric hand-dyed
by Eric Morti with resist-
dyeing by Lunn Fabrics.
Fabrics cut into directly
and machine-pieced by
Nancy Crow. Hand-quilted
by Marla Hattabaugh
with pattern denoted by
Nancy Crow.

In late January 1991, I began my first quilt in the series. As with the transitional quilts in the first chapter, I still used templates—and I still found them to be controlling. However, I did find a way to move forward. I broke down the major template shapes into secondary shapes. It was helpful to me to be able to see the actual sizes of shapes and lines translated into "tagboard" (heavy manila paper) templates. I needed to see the breakups of space before emphasizing the reconfigurations of shapes. As I worked, I was aware of a new sense of freedom . . . and an accompanying sense of awkwardness, exhilaration, and anxiety combined. Ultimately, I just wanted some kind of new freedom!

Bow Tie #4 *and* Bow Tie #5 *were a further loosening up of control. They were small studies or compositions that I planned to use as ideas for larger compositions some time down the road. Perhaps because they were so different from all of my previous work, they were quickly purchased by collectors. In retrospect, I wish I had kept them as study pieces. It has always been difficult for me to sell my work.*

# SKETCHBOOK NOTES

▼ EARLY 1991

I think every artist who succeeds (in their own terms) has some ability to keep moving forward in the face of constant obstacles . . . emotional, mental, financial, physical . . . and that is what sets them apart from all the others who have tried and quit. This is also what sets them apart from those who always talk about trying or starting but never get beyond the talking stage. I WANTED TO MOVE FORWARD, AND I WANTED TO FIND A WAY TO WORK MORE ABSTRACTLY.

▼ JANUARY 4, 1991

I have been thinking and thinking about how to proceed; how to divide up major shapes for the effect of tension. As usual I have made many possibilities out of tagboard. This helps! Now . . . I am trying to think through how I will handle the piecing and strip-piecing. Irregular? How irregular? I must keep searching nature . . . and I think the sky tonight at 11:15 P.M. may have given me my answer. To move values in and out. To move values as shapes in and out. I suspect this was a very, very important idea to the impressionists. I plan to use lush shades of red floating on the surface.

▼ MAY 6, 1991

I stayed up all night to finish *Bow Tie #2* and *Bow Tie #3* so that I can send them off to Marla to be hand-quilted. Tomorrow I leave to teach in New Zealand.

▼ RIGHT *Bow Tie #6 (1992) was based on* Bow Tie #2 *and* Bow Tie #3, *but I used a different color palette of solids. Changing color palettes has been an essential way for me to keep learning—and to keep from being bored. Color has always been comforting to me. It makes me feel safe. Color caresses my feelings and I love to be caressed and comforted.* Bow Tie #7, Bow Tie #8, *and* Bow Tie #9 *(1991–1992) were, like some of the transitional quilts in the first chapter, another attempt to incorporate commercial prints along with solids into compositions. I worked as freely as possible while still using a ruler or templates to cut edges. Skewing shapes was an important part of the freeing-up process in these three quilts.* ABOVE *Sketchbook note, dated January 4, 1991.*

*Bow Tie #6*, ©1992.
71″ × 71″. 100 percent
cotton fabric hand-dyed by
Eric Morti and Nancy Crow.
Machine-pieced by
Nancy Crow. Hand-quilted
by Marla Hattabaugh
with pattern denoted by
Nancy Crow.

*Bow Tie #7*, ©1991–1992.
31″ × 38″. 100 percent
commercial cottons.
Fabrics cut into directly
and machine-pieced by
Nancy Crow. Hand-quilted
by Marla Hattabaugh
with pattern denoted by
Nancy Crow.

*Bow Tie #8*, ©1991–1992.
35″ × 40″. 100 percent
cotton fabric hand-dyed
by Nancy Crow, plus
100 percent commercial
cottons. Fabrics cut into
directly and machine-
pieced by Nancy Crow.
Hand-quilted by Marla
Hattabaugh with pattern
denoted by Nancy Crow.

*Bow Tie #9*, ©1991–1992. 43" × 51½". 100 percent cotton fabric hand-dyed by Nancy Crow, plus 100 percent commercial cottons. Fabrics cut into directly and machine-pieced by Nancy Crow. Hand-quilted by Marla Hattabaugh with pattern denoted by Nancy Crow.

*I still love* Bow Tie #9 *because of the orange-red color I dyed and because of the use of a hand block-printed fabric I over-dyed with red.*

ABOVE *I work on multiple quilts simultaneously, ideas jumping from one quilt in the series to another. Here,* Bow Tie #7, Bow Tie #8, Bow Tie #9, Bow Tie #14, Bow Tie #15, *and* Bow Tie #16 *are in various stages of completion on the east wall of my main work area, Studio #1. The photo was taken in January 1992, but all of these quilts were started in 1991.* Bow Tie #14, Bow Tie #15, *and* Bow Tie #16 *ended the series. I had finally run out of steam.*

*Bow Tie #14*, ©1992–1997.
33″ × 35″. 100 percent
commercial cottons.
Fabrics cut into directly
and machine-pieced by
Nancy Crow. Hand-quilted
by Marla Hattabaugh
with pattern denoted by
Nancy Crow.

Bow Tie #10 (1994–1995) was a "coming of age" for me. It was started in December 1994 and I finished the machine-piecing in April 1995. From 1990 onwards, in every free minute I had, I joyfully pumped out an ever-growing stack of hand-dyed fabrics. The incredible range of colors and values led me to approach my huge work wall in a new and different manner. I selected a beginning palette and started cutting freehand with no final plan except for using a rough cut of the Bow Tie configuration I had used in Bow Tie #2, Bow Tie #3, and Bow Tie #6. I did not want templates to control any of my movements or shapes. I wanted to cut out pure shapes, pin them to my wall, then step back, letting my feelings, gut instincts, and eye take me wherever they wanted to go. Cutting a shape and paying attention to its "edge" or "line" was becoming more and more important to me. I wanted to train my eye to be "dead-on" in its decision making and in creating figure/ground relationships. For Bow Tie #10, I started by cutting random triangles, lopped off squares and rectangles . . . just trying to enjoy cutting shapes freely. One gets lost in one's thoughts during this process . . . integrated . . . that's it!

*Bow Tie #10*, ©1994–1995.
66″ × 70″. 100 percent
cotton fabric hand-dyed
by Nancy Crow. Fabrics cut
into directly and machine-
pieced by Nancy Crow.
Hand-quilted by Marla
Hattabaugh with pattern
denoted by Nancy Crow.

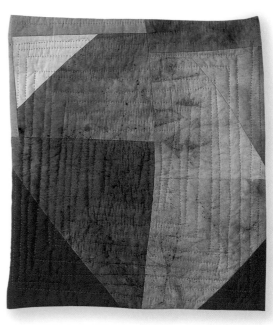

**Bow Tie #11**, ©1995. 11⅝″ × 13⅜″. 100 percent cotton fabric hand-dyed by Nancy Crow. Fabrics cut into directly and machine-pieced by Nancy Crow. Hand-quilted by Marla Hattabaugh with pattern denoted by Nancy Crow.

**Bow Tie #12**, ©1995. 28″ × 28¾″. 100 percent cotton fabric hand-dyed by Nancy Crow. Fabrics cut into directly and machine-pieced by Nancy Crow. Hand-quilted by Marla Hattabaugh with pattern denoted by Nancy Crow.

*Bow Tie #13*, ©1995.
30" × 36". 100 percent
cotton fabric hand-dyed
by Nancy Crow. Fabrics cut
into directly and machine-
pieced by Nancy Crow.
Hand-quilted by Marie
Moore with pattern
denoted by Nancy Crow.

Bow Tie #11 *came together fast. I cut the first shape, the*
*yellow shape, and added a few more shapes, and it was*
*completed. From there I moved very quickly to* Bow Tie #12
*and* Bow Tie #13. *I love the energy of all three of these quilts.*

Bow Tie #13 *is pinned on top of* Color Blocks #69 *on the large north wall of Studio #1. The quilt had just been returned from hand-quilter Marie Moore, and the batting still shows around the edge, as the quilt was not yet bound.*

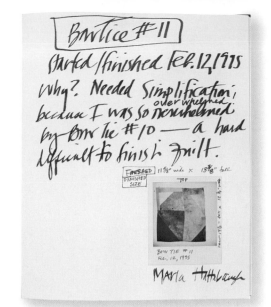

## SKETCHBOOK NOTES

▼ DECEMBER 23, 1994

Just know I am skipping around as I always seem to do. My thoughts just go where they want . . . until I STOP! In this case, until I sit STILL on top of my cutting table and try to be logical. I mean I stop all my thoughts and try to concentrate on one thing . . . right now BOW TIE! How can I capture my thoughts in color and shape about *Bow Tie* . . . and why, for Pete's sake!? I wish I could work in pastel and paper cut-outs . . . those media draw me but I don't have expertise . . . Should I stop and try?? Off the subject again and I'll tell you why . . . because I started looking at Degas' paintings as soon as I stood up. The texture in the Degas' pastels is so rich.

▼ DECEMBER 26, 1994

I asked "why?" About *Bow Tie.* I know why . . . it's those strange reactions in the corners . . . those interactions. Places to play! What type of play? I am starting with pastel colors . . . trying to lighten and change my palette. Trying hard not to use much red, red-orange, orange red—my favorites! Yes, my favorites.

▼ 1995

If one begins to be bored, disinterested in producing more work in the same vein or series, one either quits or forges ahead in a new direction . . . or comes back to the same theme later in one's career.

LEFT AND ABOVE RIGHT *I made only a few sketches while working on the Bow Tie series. Looking back at my notebooks forcefully reminds me of the constant struggle to break free.*

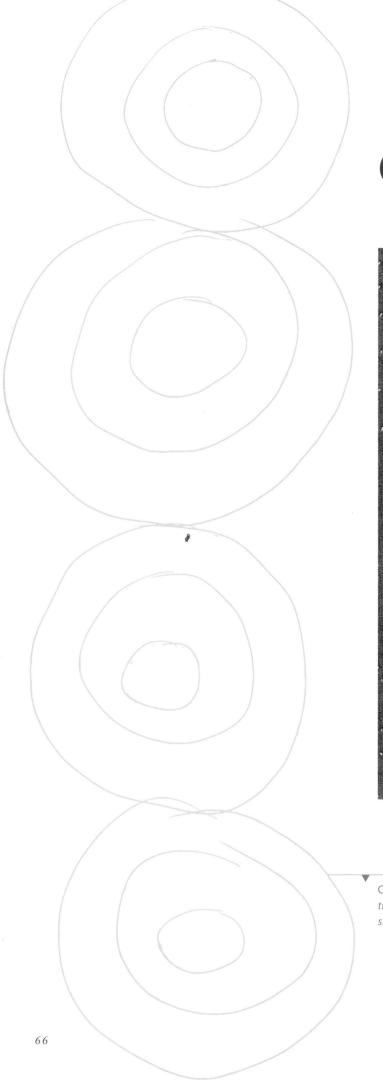

# CHINESE SOULS

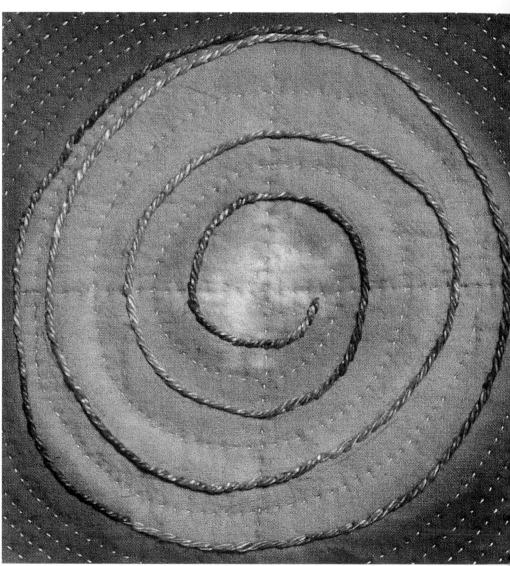

Chinese Souls #1, *started in China in September 1990, became the study for the rest of this series.* LEFT *A detail from an early sketch for Chinese Souls.*

***Chinese Souls #1,*** ©1990.
17½″ × 18″. 100 percent
cotton resist-dyed by Lunn
Fabrics. Hand-embroidered
by Nancy Crow, hand-quilted
by Kris Doyle with pattern
denoted by Nancy Crow.

*Chinese Souls #2*, ©1992.
90″ × 82″. 100 percent cotton
hand-dyed by Nancy Crow,
then resist-dyed by Lunn
Fabrics. Fabrics cut and
pieced by Nancy Crow. Hand-
embroidered by Nancy Crow,
Marla Hattabaugh, Suzanne
Keller, and Maria Magisano.
Hand-quilted by Marla
Hattabaugh with pattern
denoted by Nancy Crow.

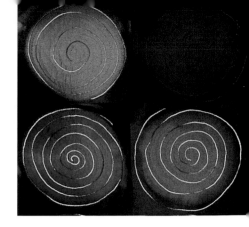

# ARTIST'S STATEMENT

IN SEPTEMBER 1990, I visited the city of Xi'an in Shaanxi Province of mainland China. While there, our interpreter took Susan Shie and me to see the famous Wild Goose Pagoda. After touring the building, we approached the exit doorway where I could hear loud police sirens booming in our direction. Suddenly two large cattle trucks came to a halt in front of us, just as we walked out of the pagoda. Police cars were leading and trailing both trucks. Startled, I noticed each truck was packed with young men standing in uncomfortable proximity to one another. Each was strung with heavy rope, hands behind his back, ropes going round and round. I frantically asked for an explanation from our interpreter but she was unyielding and said nothing. Shocked, I stared at the truck and the men. I suddenly realized how young they all were, maybe in their teens and early twenties, and they were terrified. Again, I asked what was going on. Again, she refused to tell me. But I could not look away and I could not give up asking because the men all looked to be the same age as my own sons back home. I felt sick at my stomach and asked once more: "What is going on?" With utter sadness and shame, our interpreter told me that these young men were being driven around the city of Xi'an in the trucks with sirens blaring to scare the populace out of committing crimes. Many of them, she said, had done nothing more than pick pockets. All would be executed very soon by a single shot to the base of the head. I almost fell to the ground, sick with fear and sorrow. Never had I witnessed such an atrocity. The eyes of the young men seemed to peer at me, appealing for help . . . help that I had no power to give. I wanted to flee China, to go home, to hug my own sons, to know that they were safe.

Back in my room, among my belongings I found a bag containing one small piece of tan colored fabric with a pattern of resist-dyed circles and a clump of hand-dyed embroidery flosses. I threaded my needle and began embroidering the ropes around the souls of the young men. Only this embroidery work kept me sane during the rest of the trip. I knew I could not talk with anyone

*Because* Chinese Souls #2 *was so huge, I asked three friends, Marla Hattabaugh, Suzanne Keller, and Maria Magisano, to help me embroider the ropes around the circles. There is a sense of inherent eeriness in the beauty of the quilt lines around each circle. The quilt is now in the collection of The Indianapolis Museum of Art.*

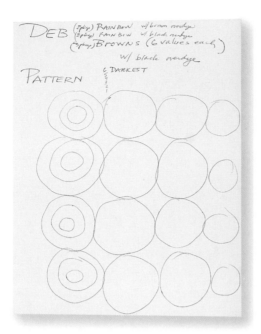

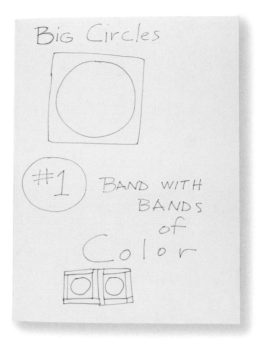

about what I had seen—it was a scene tourists were not meant to witness. This was the year after Tiananmen Square, and in the cities we traveled, fear was palpable in the air.

When I returned home, I commissioned Lunn Fabrics to resist-dye circle patterns in different sizes and colors onto fabric. I cut then lined up squares containing the circles and began to work on a group of six quilts to memorialize those Chinese souls. I kept everything very spare. As I worked in the silence of my studio, I could hear the plaintive cries of the young men. Often I had to stop working because I was crying so hard.

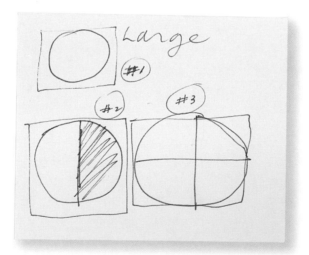

TOP *Early sketches for* Chinese Souls. ABOVE LEFT AND CENTER *Tail-lights on a wagon, photographed during my tour of China, and sketches reflecting those shapes.* ABOVE RIGHT *On a roadway, looking through the windscreen at a truck ahead of us, I was struck by the shapes I saw.*

Chinese Souls #1
*on my work wall.*

*Chinese Souls #3*, ©1992.
70" × 70". 100 percent cotton
hand-dyed by Eric Morti and
Nancy Crow, then resist-dyed
by Lunn Fabrics. Fabrics cut
and pieced by Nancy Crow.
Hand-quilted by Sue Milling
with pattern denoted by
Nancy Crow.

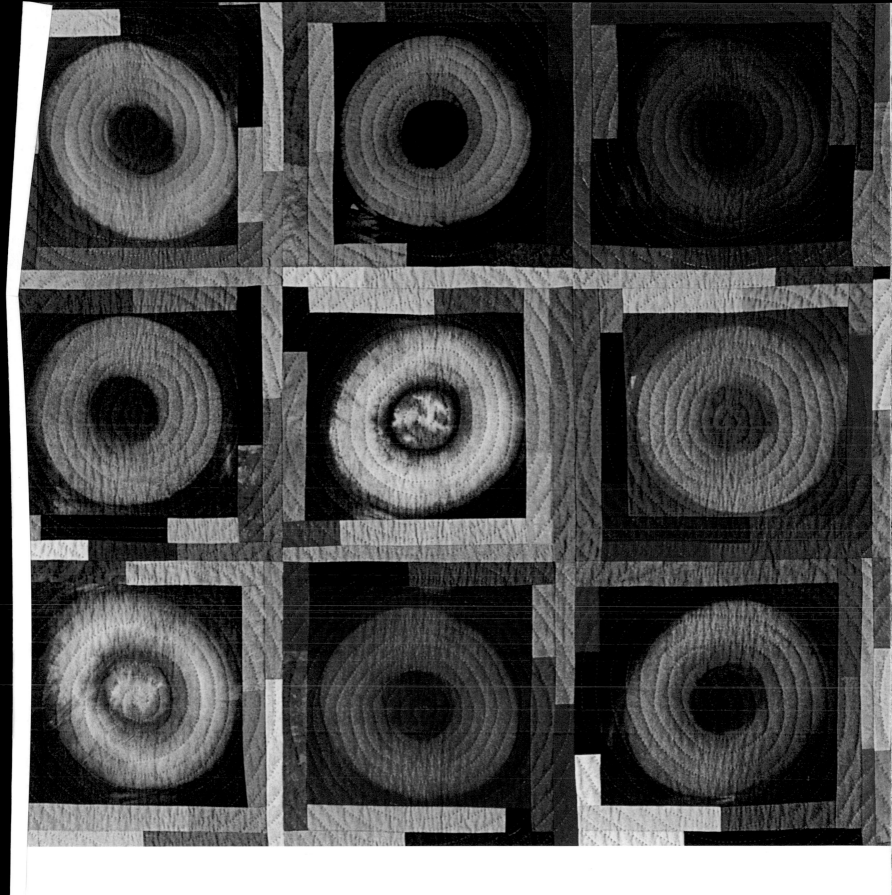

In Chinese Souls #3 (see page 72), a face seems to appear in the center of the yellow circle in the second row, third square from the left (center image in the detail above). I do not remember seeing this face before I sent the top out to be hand-quilted. When it came back, quilter Sue Milling had pinned a tiny cross on the top back of the quilt. As soon as I saw it, I knew why she had pinned it there. She had seen a "face" in one of the cloth circles. The face symbolized the souls crying out for help. Again I wept. I hung the quilt up on my work wall. Every time I went into my studio to work, I heard the voices, very soft but insistent. Finally, I had to take the quilt down, because I was haunted by the voices, and the face.

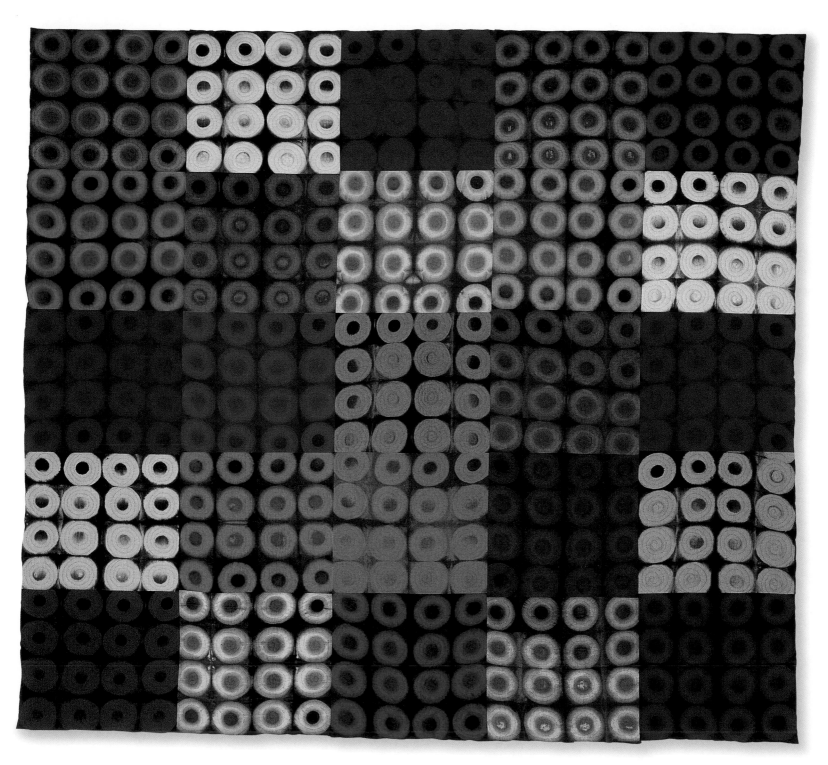

*Chinese Souls #5*, ©1992.
90" × 82". 100 percent
cotton hand-dyed by
Nancy Crow then resist-
dyed by Lunn Fabrics.
Fabrics cut and pieced
by Nancy Crow. Hand-
quilted by Marie Moore
with pattern denoted by
Nancy Crow.

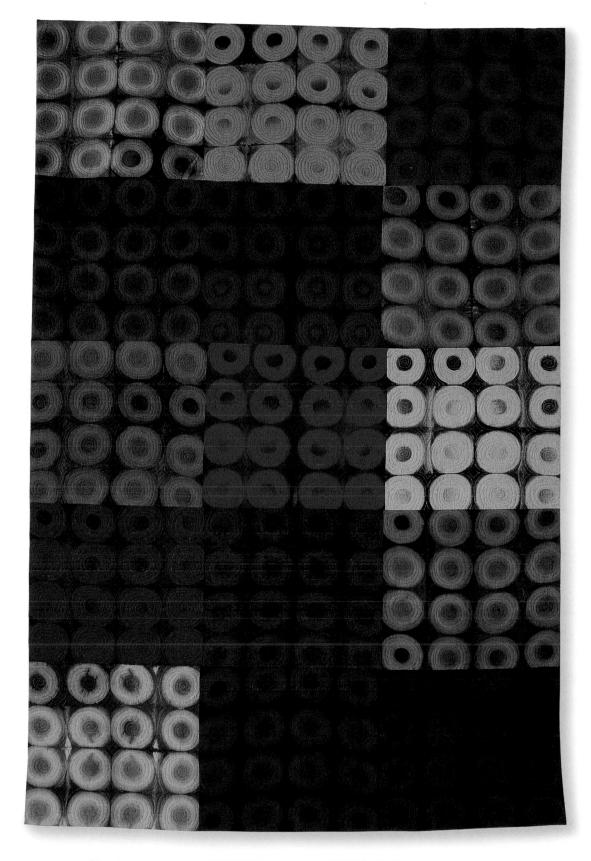

*Chinese Souls #4*, ©1992. 52¾" × 80½". 100 percent cotton resist-dyed by Lunn Fabrics. Fabrics cut and pieced by Nancy Crow. Machine-quilted by Anna Mae Gazo with pattern denoted by Nancy Crow.

RIGHT *Windows in the Forbidden City, Beijing. I love the sense of gridwork and lines, both vertical and horizontal. This format was instrumental in the design of the first six* Chinese Souls *quilts.*

# ARTIST EXCHANGE TRIP TO SHAANXI PROVINCE, CHINA

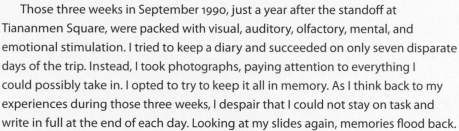

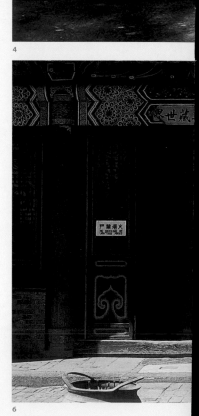

CHINA, AS IN THE HUGE, overwhelming country of China, has always mysteriously beckoned me. As an artist, I am intensely curious about the lives of fellow artists. What is it that motivates an artist? What are his or her thinking processes? Where does the artist fit in within the greater community, and is he or she necessary to the life of that community? Questions like these are particularly interesting when considering artists who live in a Communist country. What kind of spaces do artists have as their own? What materials do they use? How prolific are they? How focused? How do they view themselves and their work? I was fortunate to have an opportunity to ask and answer some of these questions. On September 10, 1990, I boarded a flight for Beijing as one of four Ohio artists selected for a three-week exchange program between the Ohio Arts Council and the Cultural Agency of Shaanxi Province in mainland China.

Those three weeks in September 1990, just a year after the standoff at Tiananmen Square, were packed with visual, auditory, olfactory, mental, and emotional stimulation. I tried to keep a diary and succeeded on only seven disparate days of the trip. Instead, I took photographs, paying attention to everything I could possibly take in. I opted to try to keep it all in memory. As I think back to my experiences during those three weeks, I despair that I could not stay on task and write in full at the end of each day. Looking at my slides again, memories flood back.

Along with my limited luggage, I brought my camera, a 35-mm Nikon with 28 mm lens and 55 mm macro lens. I packed the equipment into an airtight leather case, which I am convinced saved it from the dust that swirls in the air in Shaanxi Province. I also brought 24 rolls of Kodachrome ASA64 slide film. Another essential that I packed was a plentiful supply of Imodium A–D—our savior from food poisoning, without which we would have been bedridden for much of the trip. I regret that I did not bring one of my quilts to share with the Chinese artists I met. I was concerned—wrongly, as it turns out—that I would not be able to bring an art work through customs. (All photographs ©1990 by Nancy Crow.)

FROM TOP LEFT, PHOTO 1 *A scene I photographed in the home of mask maker Li Ji You, who lives and works in a third-floor walk-up apartment near the city of Baoji, Shaanxi Province. I saw this arrangement as beautifully spaced and full of visual information, the type of display that always attracts me—one that is, to be precise,* CHOCK-FULL OF PATTERNING! *The figure of the dog reminded me of Mexican folk art and made me wonder if there are connections between the folk arts of these two countries.* PHOTOS 2 AND 3 *The walls of every room in the mask maker's tiny apartment were totally covered with his work, with, I would guess, about 200 masks on display. They are carved out of wood, then painted. It was glorious to walk in and be surrounded by so much energy! Li Ji You was a delight—warm, charming, and constantly smiling. He loved what he was doing and seemed so happy and gregarious. I picked out three masks to buy, but Li Ji You would let me have only one of them, telling me I had chosen his three best!*

5

7

▼

PHOTO 4 *A typical tree-lined roadway. Notice the vertical lines created by the tree trunks. We spent hours driving during the trip, with our driver constantly honking as he passed bicycle riders on the road. But the panoramic sweep of the magnificent countryside more than made up for the discomfort of all the dust and noise. Also, since I am fascinated by folk art, I felt lucky to have been chosen to go "out to the villages."*
PHOTO 5 *A window filled with vertical strips of wood, which to me are similar to the vertical lines of tree trunks and which I therefore inherently love. Images like this influenced later works like* Constructions. *I see all of my work, regardless of the series, as very organic and overlapping, consistently overlapping. Looking at this image, I see the consistency of my vision and my love of particular configurations.* PHOTO 6 *A temple in China, with a lone tree in front. I like the vertical lines in this composition.* PHOTO 7 *A window in an adobe house in a pottery village. Each "pane" is filled with a paper cutout in place of glass.*

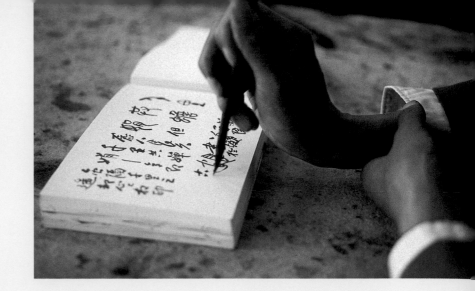

# TRAVEL JOURNAL

SEPTEMBER 12, 1990 *ARRIVING IN CHINA*

I think all of us were rather tense on arrival. In my case, I was dealing with all my preconceptions of what China must be like, and thoughts like "police state" kept going through my mind. I was worried that no one would meet us at the airport and we would not find our way to our hotel. . . . Since it was already dark when we left the airport, I found the long drive somewhat eerie. All we could see ahead was a road lined by trees on both sides. We could see nothing of the countryside . . . and very few vehicles of any kind except an occasional bicycle. The streetlights had very dull bulbs. I kept thinking, "Where are we?" We might have been anywhere in the world, as it did not seem particularly Chinese. It was nothing like Hong Kong with its cars, cars, cars.

SEPTEMBER 16 *QIAN-YANG CITY, SHAANXI PROVINCE*

Left alone with free time, we walked to the Shaanxi Municipal Museum, finding our own way through the throngs of Chinese crowding the narrow streets. I was fascinated with the calligraphy I noticed on shop signs, with so much of the lettering done freehand.

SEPTEMBER 18 *QIAN-YANG CITY, SHAANXI PROVINCE*

While walking back up the four flights of stairs to my hotel room after a banquet in our honor, I decided to go out on the balcony to observe the balconies of the apartment buildings surrounding our hotel. Every balcony was crammed . . . with plants, in lieu of a backyard or garden, with clothes drying on lines, with boxes stacked high. I noticed the odor of coal smoke, which becomes stronger in the evenings when people are cooking, and I noticed that I could not see stars or the moon. In fact, the whole time I was in China, I did not once see stars or the moon. That is how polluted it is due to all the coal smoke . . . and dust that blows around in the air.

ABOVE RIGHT *Zhao Bu Tang at work. This calligrapher has a wonderful sense of positive/negative space and composition. It was truly a pleasure to watch him. I think it must be very important for a calligrapher to be absolutely sensitive to filling the negative space.* RIGHT *I love this photo of craftsman Du Ying with his grandchild hovering by his knee. It signifies for me the way an artist's life should be—total integration of work and family life.*

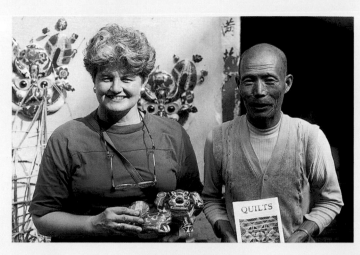

TOP *About 40 kilometers outside Baoji, we stopped at the pottery village of Liu Ying and visited the Fengxiang country artisans.* ABOVE *Potter Hu Shen works on folk sculptures for festivals. The internal structures of the larger sculptures are made out of wood lathe. Again I was struck by the similarity to Mexican folk art.*

My fellow artist Susan Shie and I visited a village where local embroiderers crowded into the community center to hear our presentations. We were so enthusiastically received it seemed the whole village had turned out for us, with children sitting in the open windows. Susan and I were true curiosities, and the older women wanted to hold our hands or stroke our skin. We noticed that many of them had tiny feet that were so distorted from being bound as babies that they had difficulty walking.

Later, three of the best embroiderers were invited to our hotel to join us for a "sewing bee." We set up tables, and a treadle sewing machine was brought in for me to use. All the other women, including Susan, sewed by hand. With the help of our interpreter, we slowly became acquainted. The women had brought large amounts of textiles with them and they put up a handsome and interesting display all around the room. The sewing bee was memorable for me because I just love observing how others behave. These women were so focused and determined to get all their blocks done in the time we had allotted. And only a fellow needleworker knows the enormous amount of time that sewing takes. The women enjoyed interacting with us—and they loved having Susan and me make a fuss over their work! We continued sewing until all the projects were finished and we had enough quilt blocks to exchange with each other.

It rained hard. Poured. As I stared out the window into the street below, I heard music, strange music, coming closer, almost like wailing. Soon I saw a procession, a burial procession with trumpeters in front and at the end. Everyone was dressed in white, and the coffin was carried on the shoulders of men. It was all so archaic, so mysterious, and the rain was falling so hard. I felt strange.

TOP *Students at the Xi'an Fine Arts Academy crowd around me for a demonstration.*

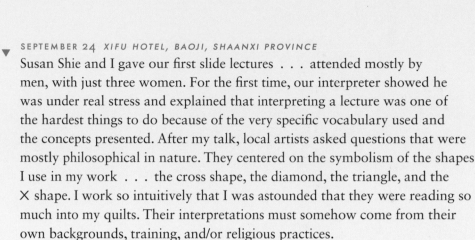

**SEPTEMBER 24** *XIFU HOTEL, BAOJI, SHAANXI PROVINCE*

Susan Shie and I gave our first slide lectures . . . attended mostly by men, with just three women. For the first time, our interpreter showed he was under real stress and explained that interpreting a lecture was one of the hardest things to do because of the very specific vocabulary used and the concepts presented. After my talk, local artists asked questions that were mostly philosophical in nature. They centered on the symbolism of the shapes I use in my work . . . the cross shape, the diamond, the triangle, and the X shape. I work so intuitively that I was astounded that they were reading so much into my quilts. Their interpretations must somehow come from their own backgrounds, training, and/or religious practices.

**SEPTEMBER 25** *XI'AN, SHAANXI PROVINCE*

In lieu of a clock or alarm, loudspeakers started blasting every morning at 6:30 A.M. The most awful music! It was absolutely impossible to sleep, as the music went on for the next half hour. We noticed that groups of students did aerobic workouts to the music out on the streets, or jogged to it. Loudspeakers are attached to nearly every telephone and electricity pole around the city.

**SEPTEMBER 27** *XI'AN, SHAANXI PROVINCE*

In the morning we visited the Department of Traditional Chinese Painting at Xi'an Fine Arts Academy and also saw classes in design. I found this very, very interesting and came away feeling that the students were well-trained. The drawing classes were terrific. . . . In the afternoon, we visited the Department of Arts and Crafts and there I was disappointed. The work seemed so outdated.

**SEPTEMBER 30** *XI'AN, SHAANXI PROVINCE*

We spent the whole morning and part of the early afternoon giving demonstrations of our work to students at the Xi'an Fine Arts Academy. I made part of a small quilt and shared a stack of textile magazines with the students. They devoured everything. I wish we could have spent three to four days working as artists-in-residence and at the same time have an exhibition of our work. I think it would have been a revelation for both the students and the faculty. As it was, I feel none of them had a good grasp of what we were all about . . . or why we were making quilts, of all things! Tomorrow, we begin the long journey home via Guangzhou and Hong Kong.

**ABOVE** *Folk artist Ma Leimei holds one of the toys she creates, made from cotton and richly embroidered. Ma Leimei was so gentle, charming, and warm—a first-class human being.*
**LEFT** *I love this image of Ma Leimei's hands.*

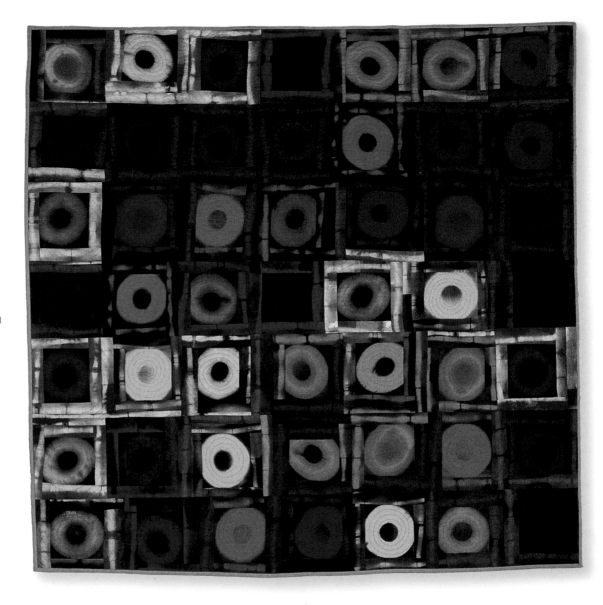

*Chinese Souls #6*, ©1992. 43¾" × 43¾". 100 percent cotton hand-dyed by Nancy Crow then resist-dyed by Lunn Fabrics. Fabrics cut and pieced by Nancy Crow. Hand-quilted by Mary Underwood with pattern denoted by Nancy Crow.

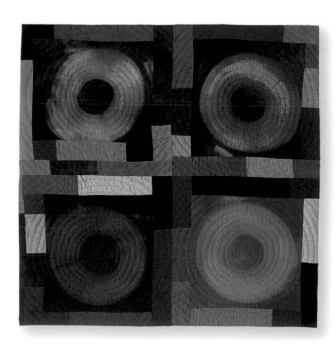

*Chinese Souls #7*, ©1993. 22" × 22". 100 percent cotton hand-dyed by Nancy Crow with circles resist-dyed by Lunn Fabrics. Fabrics cut and pieced by Nancy Crow. Machine-quilted by Kris Doyle with pattern denoted by Nancy Crow.

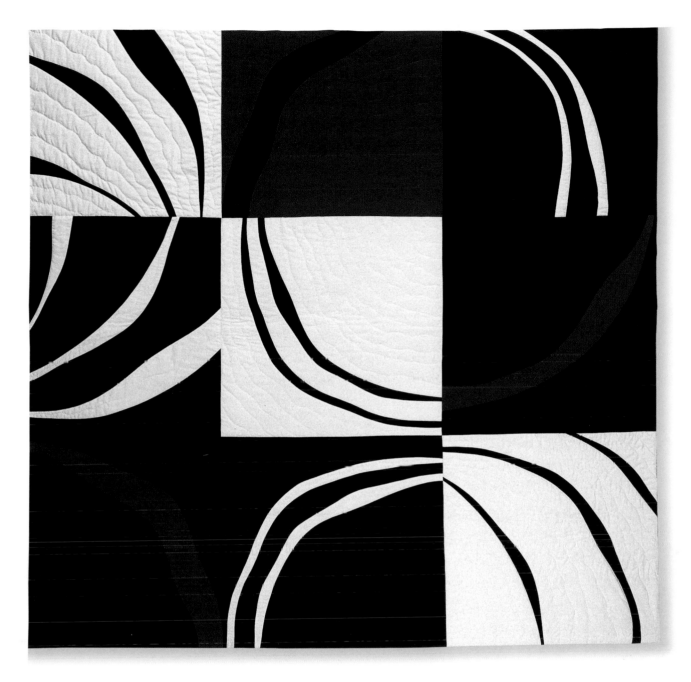

*Chinese Souls #10,* ©1994. 56″ × 56″. 100 percent cotton. Red fabric hand-dyed by Nancy Crow. Fabrics cut and pieced by Nancy Crow. Machine-quilted by Marla Hattabaugh with pattern denoted by Nancy Crow.

Chinese Souls #10 *came later, three years later, and is a more elegant rendering of the ropes around the souls. I wanted utter simplicity, spareness, and few colors, just those so commonly seen in China.* LEFT *Stacked ceramic tiles I saw during the visit to China. I took this photo because I love the repetition.*

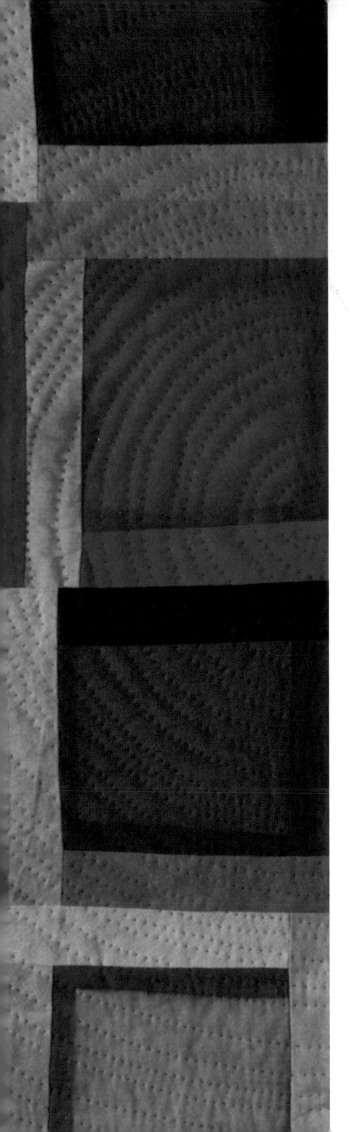

# COLOR BLOCKS II

*Color Blocks #16*, ©1991.
50" × 44". 100 percent
cotton fabrics hand-dyed by
Eric Morti and Nancy Crow.
Resist-dyed cottons by Lunn
Fabrics. Fabrics cut into
directly and machine-pieced
by Nancy Crow. Hand-quilted
by Kris Doyle with pattern
denoted by Nancy Crow.
At left, *Color Blocks #17*, detail.

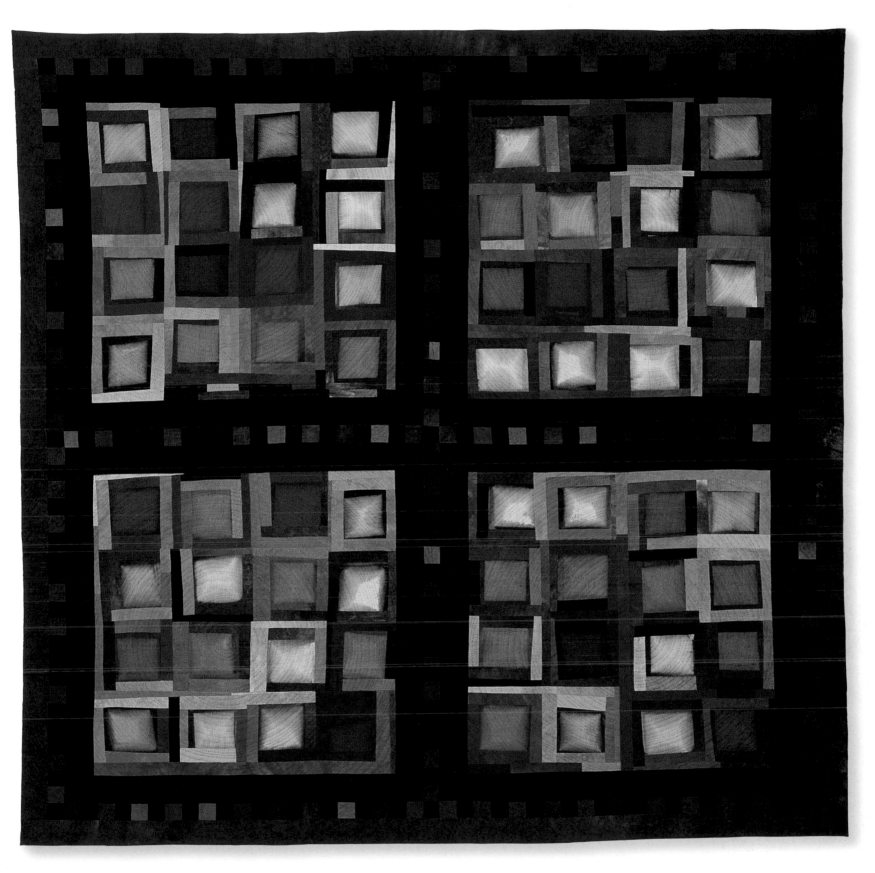

*Color Blocks #17*, ©1991–1992. 71½" × 71½". 100 percent cotton fabrics hand-dyed by Eric Morti and Nancy Crow. Resist-dyed cottons by Lunn Fabrics. Fabrics cut into directly and machine-pieced by Nancy Crow. Hand-quilted by Brenda Stultz with pattern denoted by Nancy Crow.

*Color Blocks #17*, back view.

# ARTIST'S STATEMENT

WITH *COLOR BLOCKS #15* (see page 45), I felt I had made a breakthrough. As I moved on with the series I became consumed by it. Ideas flooded my brain, overwhelming me with possibilities, pushing me to make quilt after quilt. The one-patch format became ever more elaborate, yet freer. At times I created quilts very similar in nature, and then I just as abruptly veered off into other directions. As long as the concept of Color Blocks drove my ideas, all of these quilts were grouped together, no matter how much or how little they seem to be related. I continued to work on them through 1995, and then off and on until 1997. As explained later in this chapter, there were two primary visual influences on the series. The first influence, particularly evident in *Color Blocks #22*, *Color Blocks #26*, and *Color Blocks #27*, (see pages 97, 103, and 105) came from doors that I saw and photographed during a 1993 visit to Guatemala. The second came from two antique Log Cabin quilts in my collection.

Most, but not all, of the *Color Blocks* quilts have been hand-quilted in a circular design that was taken from my *Chinese Souls* series. I found that I liked the visual tension and energy these circular patterns created on top of the pieced, angular, square formats beneath.

From *Color Blocks #15* all the way up through *Color Blocks #40*, the compositions were certainly closely related. The exception is *Color Blocks #21*, which eventually became the idea behind *Color Blocks #58* (see page 127).

With *Color Blocks #41* (see page 116) I veered off into other experimentation, attempting to cut freely and directly into my fabrics, working on intuition, working improvisationally. I approached each composition with no planning, no idea of what might happen. I embraced the idea that ART WAS A PROCESS OF DISCOVERY, that for me the freshest ideas, the most interesting ideas, came about by observing shapes and lines that had been cut, then

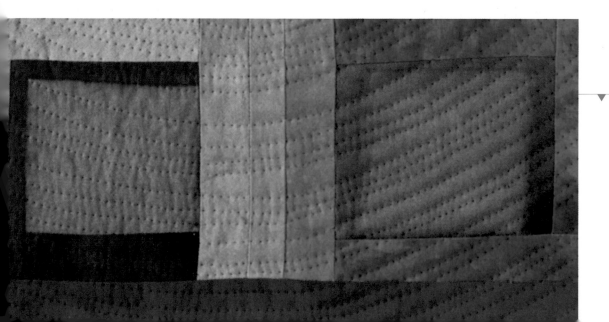

*Most of the quilts in my Color Blocks series are quilted in a circular design, as these two details from Color Blocks #17 show.*

pinned to the wall. With practice, I came to believe those shapes and lines and their spatial relationships would lead the way if I could relax enough to allow this to happen. It meant I became more vigilant about keeping "the critic" in me at bay until I was ready to do the refining before sewing. This meant I had to learn to trust my instincts, to believe in my own eye and its ability to recognize strong composition. And it meant I had to be able to deal with plenty of disappointment and failed compositions.

I was excited! I made study after study, each different. I just wanted to experiment. And with the experimenting, I found my hand, wrist, and arm muscles becoming stronger and stronger as I became more sensitive to how I cut edges . . . edges of shapes and lines. Of course, I went backwards at times, recreating quilts or creating similar quilts to those I had made in 1992 and 1993, but I saw everything I made as compositional practice. And machine-piecing kept me sane and steady through stressful times.

By 1994, I had produced a solid enough body of work to land, with the help of Penny McMorris, a one-artist exhibition at The Renwick Gallery of the Museum of American Art, Smithsonian Institution, Washington, D.C. The exhibition ran from August 25, 1995 to January 1, 1996 and was accompanied by a catalog, titled *Improvisational Quilts*. Seeing my quilts made from 1988 to 1995 hang in the Renwick galleries gave me the very rare opportunity to actually study my work as a body and to examine and think about the quality of the work I had achieved. One thing I knew in my heart was that my "eye" was getting better and better.

As I study the quilts I made in 1994 and 1995, I see now that they were preparation for my journey into creating the largest series of my career . . . *Constructions*.

LEFT *Working in my sketchbook in Studio #1.*

ABOVE Color Blocks #20 *under construction in Studio #1 in 1992.* LEFT Color Blocks #19 *relates to the small study* Color Blocks #34 *(see page 112).*

***Color Blocks #19***, ©1992.
75″ × 75″. 100 percent
cotton fabrics hand-dyed
by Nancy Crow. Fabrics cut
and machine-pieced by
Nancy Crow. Hand-quilted
by Marla Hattabaugh
with pattern denoted by
Nancy Crow.

*Color Blocks #18*,
©1991–1992. 32″ × 49″.
100 percent cotton
fabrics hand-dyed by
Nancy Crow. Resist-
dyed cottons by Lunn
Fabrics. Fabrics cut into
directly and machine-
pieced by Nancy Crow.
Hand-quilted by Gail
Chatterson with pattern
denoted by Nancy Crow.
Opposite page, detail,
*Color Blocks #18*.

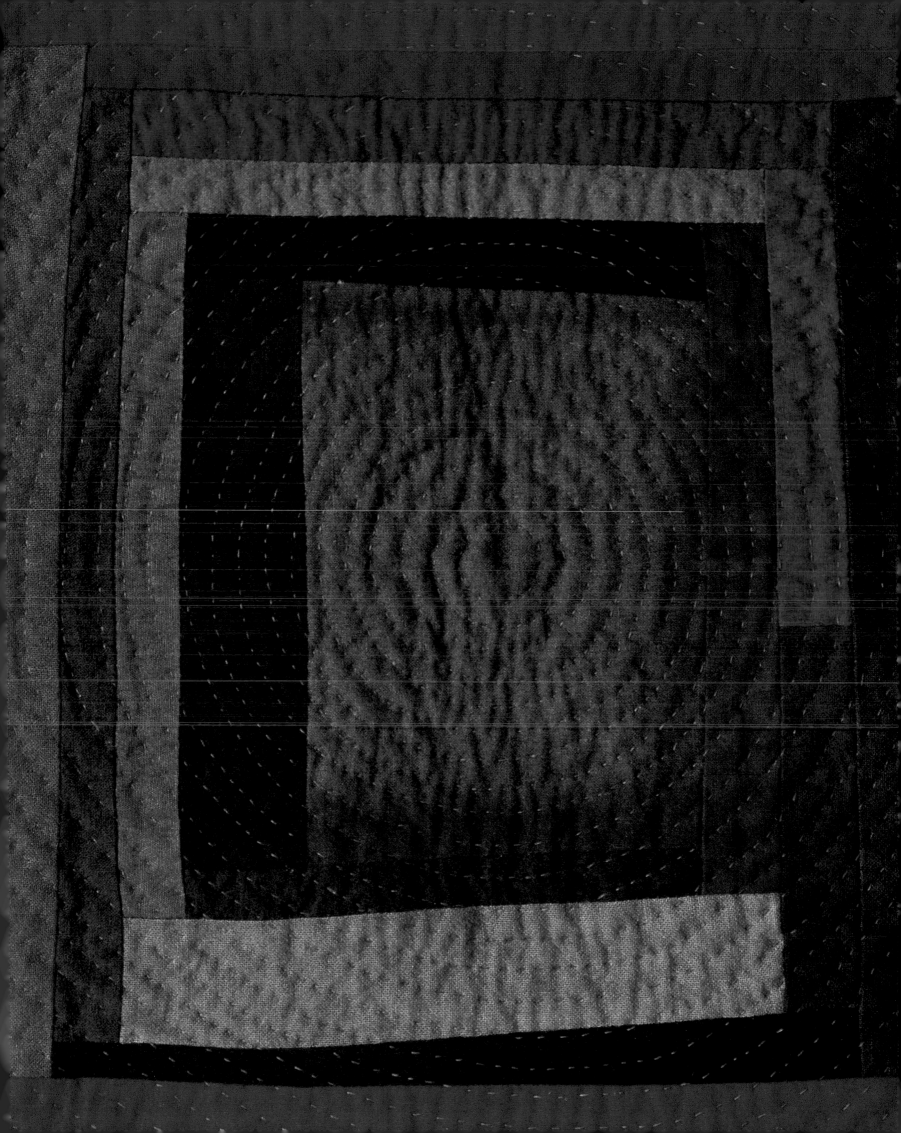

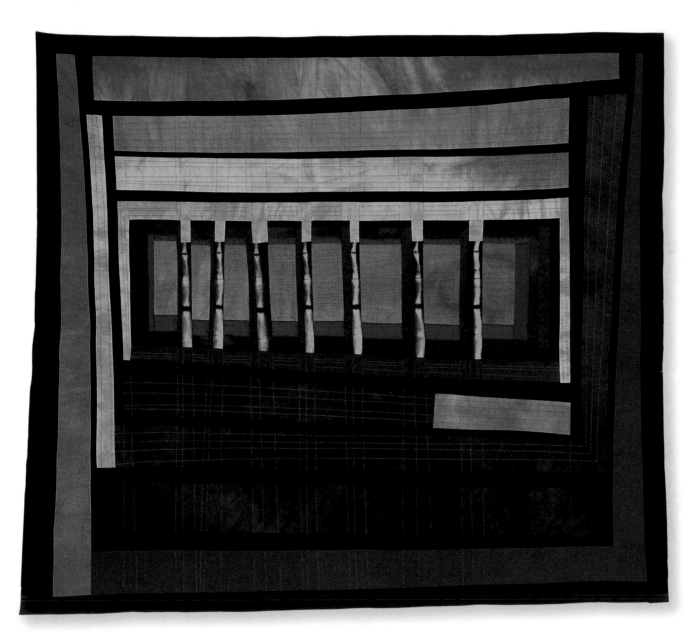

*Color Blocks #21*, ©1992. 46½″ × 41½″. 100 percent cotton fabrics hand-dyed by Nancy Crow then resist-dyed by Lunn Fabrics. Fabrics cut into directly and machine-pieced by Nancy Crow. Hand-quilted by Kris Doyle with pattern denoted by Nancy Crow.

Color Blocks #21 *relates to a later work,* Color Blocks #58 *(see page 127).*

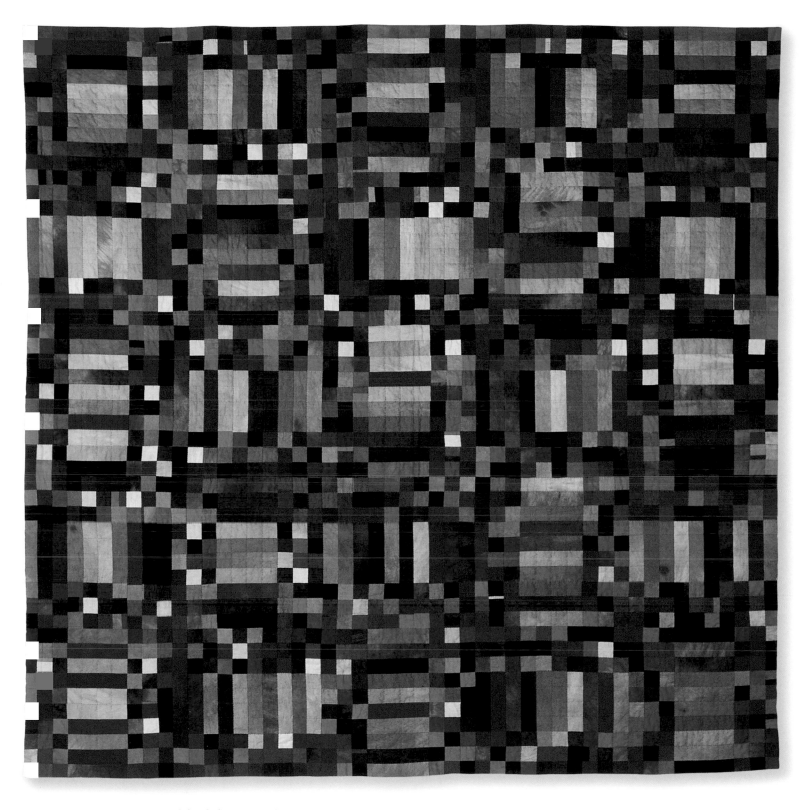

*Color Blocks #20*, ©1992.
72" × 72". 100 percent
cotton fabrics hand-dyed
by Nancy Crow. Fabrics cut
and machine-pieced by
Nancy Crow. Hand-quilted
by Sue Milling with pattern
denoted by Nancy Crow.

# GUATEMALA DOORS

I TOOK ALL OF THESE PHOTOS during a visit to Guatemala in August 1993. These images influenced my color choices and ideas for the *Color Blocks* series. The same visual impact is evident in many of the quilts, particularly in *Color Blocks #22, Color Blocks #26,* and *Color Blocks #27* (see pages 97, 103, and 105).

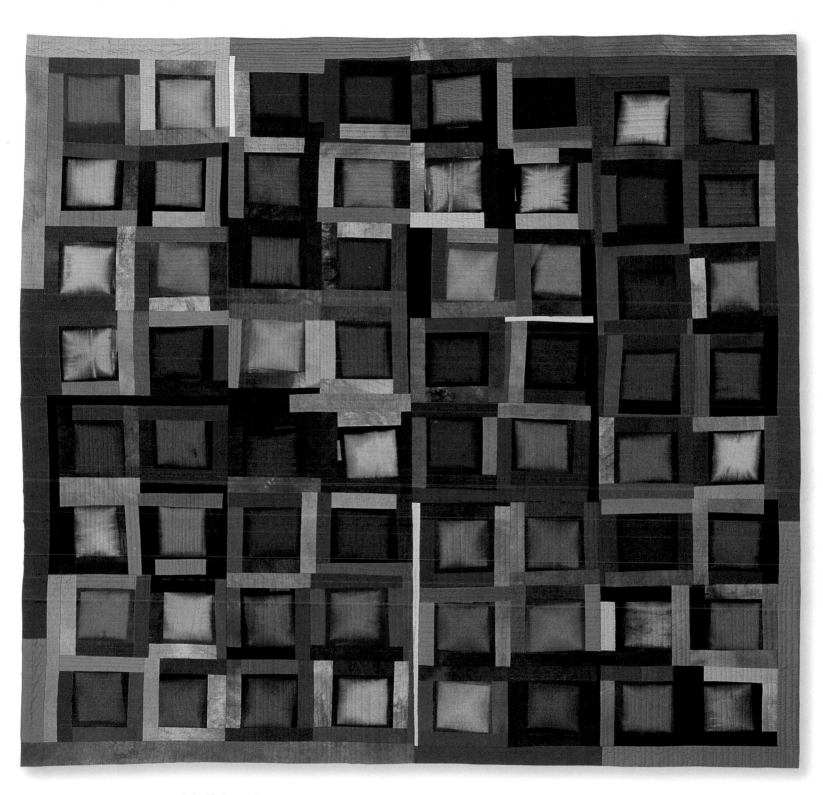

***Color Blocks #22***, ©1992.
73″ × 73″. 100 percent
cotton fabrics hand-dyed
by Nancy Crow then resist-
dyed by Lunn Fabrics.
Fabrics cut into directly
and machine-pieced
by Nancy Crow. Hand-
quilted by Marie Moore
with pattern denoted by
Nancy Crow.

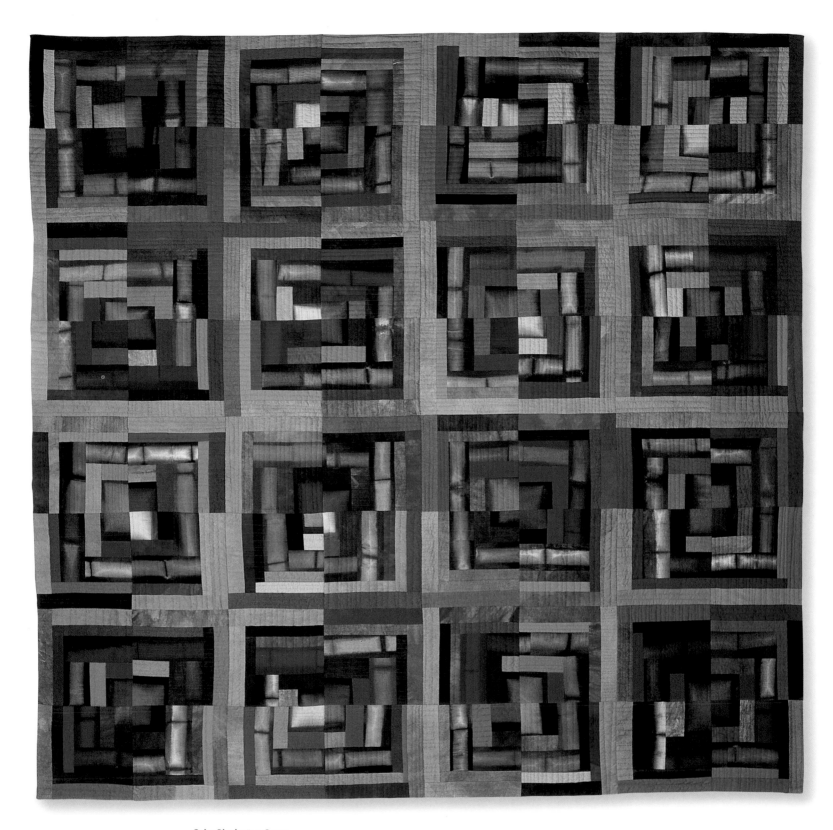

*Color Blocks #23*, ©1992.
72" × 72". 100 percent
cotton fabrics hand-dyed by
Nancy Crow then resist-dyed
by Lunn Fabrics. Fabrics cut
into directly and machine-
pieced by Nancy Crow. Hand-
quilted by Marla Hattabaugh
with pattern denoted by
Nancy Crow.

***Color Blocks #24***, ©1992.
72" × 72". 100 percent
cotton fabrics hand-dyed
by Nancy Crow then resist-
dyed by Lunn Fabrics.
Fabrics cut into directly
and machine-pieced by
Nancy Crow. Hand-quilted
by Kris Doyle with pattern
denoted by Nancy Crow.

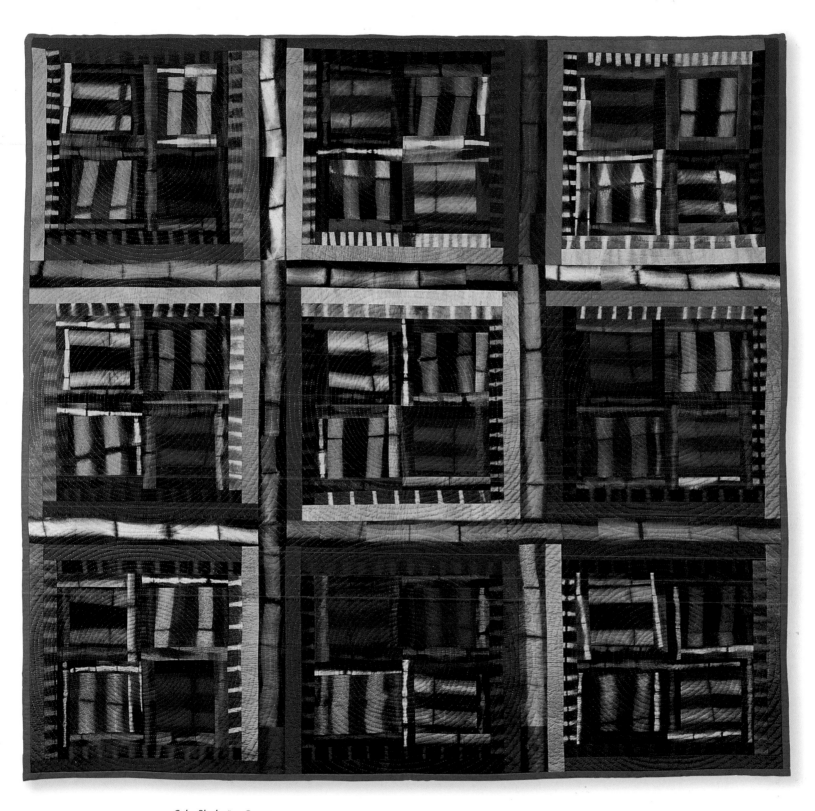

***Color Blocks #25***, ©1992.
68″ × 68″. 100 percent
cotton fabrics hand-dyed
by Nancy Crow then resist-
dyed by Lunn Fabrics.
Fabrics cut into directly
and machine-pieced
by Nancy Crow. Hand-
quilted by Marie Moore
with pattern denoted by
Nancy Crow.

ABOVE Color Blocks #26 *under construction in Studio #1 in May 1992.*

***Color Blocks #26***, ©1992.
64″ × 64″. 100 percent
cotton fabrics hand-dyed
by Nancy Crow then resist-
dyed by Lunn Fabrics.
Fabrics cut into directly
and machine-pieced
by Nancy Crow. Hand-
quilted by Brenda Stultz
with pattern denoted by
Nancy Crow.

*Color Blocks #27*, ©1992.
68″ × 68″. 100 percent
cotton fabrics hand-dyed
by Nancy Crow then resist-
dyed by Lunn Fabrics.
Fabrics cut into directly
and machine-pieced by
Nancy Crow. Hand-quilted
by Marla Hattabaugh
with pattern denoted by
Nancy Crow.

*Log Cabin*, ca. 1880s.
78" × 78". Linen, wool,
silk, and homespun
cotton. Hand-pieced by
Huldah Rachel Brown.
Collection of Nancy Crow.

# ANTIQUE LOG CABINS

IN SOME OF THE *Color Blocks* quilts, I introduced Log Cabin variations because I have always loved the old Log Cabin quilts. I have two very fine antique Log Cabin quilts in my collection. The first was made in the 1800s by my maternal great-grandmother Huldah Rachel Brown. It is made of linen, wool, silk, and homespun cotton. My great-grandmother cut very fine logs or strips and hand-pieced those to a backing. This quilt was presented to me by my cousin Betty Bender and her husband Gene George.

I purchased the other Log Cabin quilt, made sometime in the 1880s, because I was impressed by the fineness of its logs or strips. It is made of wool and silk. Its maker managed to create the wonderful sense of a large linear drawing. From a distance, one almost does not know it is a quilt. This linear sensibility influenced me to try sewing very fine strips around the squares in *Color Blocks #16*, *Color Blocks #17*, and *Color Blocks #18* (see pages 84, 85, and 90). The photographs are © by J. Kevin Fitzsimons.

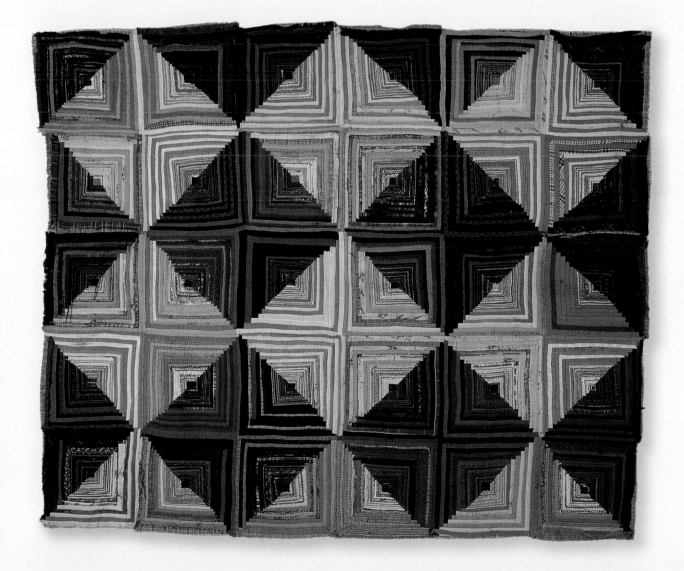

*Log Cabin*, ca. 1880s. 90″ × 75″. Wool and silk. Hand-pieced, maker unknown. Collection of Nancy Crow.

*Color Blocks #28*, ©1992.
68" × 88". 100 percent
cotton fabrics hand-dyed
by Nancy Crow then resist-
dyed by Lunn Fabrics.
Fabrics cut into directly
and machine-pieced by
Nancy Crow. Hand-quilted
by Marla Hattabaugh
with pattern denoted by
Nancy Crow.

*Color Blocks #29*, ©1992. 53″ × 53″. 100 percent cotton fabrics hand-dyed by Nancy Crow then resist-dyed by Lunn Fabrics. Fabrics cut into directly and machine-pieced by Nancy Crow. Hand-quilted by Sue Milling with pattern denoted by Nancy Crow.

*Color Blocks #30*, ©1992. 46″ × 46″. 100 percent cotton fabrics hand-dyed by Nancy Crow then resist-dyed by Lunn Fabrics. Fabrics cut into directly and machine-pieced by Nancy Crow. Hand-quilted by Kris Doyle with pattern denoted by Nancy Crow.

*Color Blocks #34*, ©1993.
29″ × 21½″. 100 percent
cotton fabrics hand-dyed
by Nancy Crow. Fabrics cut
into directly and machine-
pieced by Nancy Crow.
Hand-quilted by Kris Doyle
with pattern denoted by
Nancy Crow.

*Color Blocks #35*, ©1993.
34½″ × 36½″. 100 percent
cotton fabrics hand-dyed
by Nancy Crow then resist-
dyed by Lunn Fabrics.
Fabrics cut into directly
and machine-pieced
by Nancy Crow. Hand-
quilted by Marie Moore
with pattern denoted by
Nancy Crow.

ABOVE Color Blocks #35 *relates to Color Blocks #71 (see page 135) and to Constructions #15 (see page 192).* LEFT *I bought this antique quilt for the cross motif, since I had used this motif on and off in earlier works. Color Blocks #35 has a cross shape at the center, just as this one does.*

*Color Blocks #33*, ©1993.
66" × 48". 100 percent
cotton fabrics hand-dyed
by Nancy Crow then resist-
dyed by Lunn Fabrics.
Fabrics cut into directly
and machine-pieced by
Nancy Crow. Hand-quilted
by Marla Hattabaugh
with pattern denoted by
Nancy Crow.

*Color Blocks #31*, ©1992. 22″ × 22″. 100 percent cotton fabrics hand-dyed by Nancy Crow then resist-dyed by Lunn Fabrics. Fabrics cut into directly and machine-pieced by Nancy Crow. Hand-quilted by Marie Moore with pattern denoted by Nancy Crow.

*Color Blocks #32*, ©1992. 41½″ × 42″. 100 percent cotton fabrics hand-dyed by Nancy Crow then resist-dyed by Lunn Fabrics. Fabrics cut into directly and machine-pieced by Nancy Crow. Hand-quilted by Kris Doyle with pattern denoted by Nancy Crow.

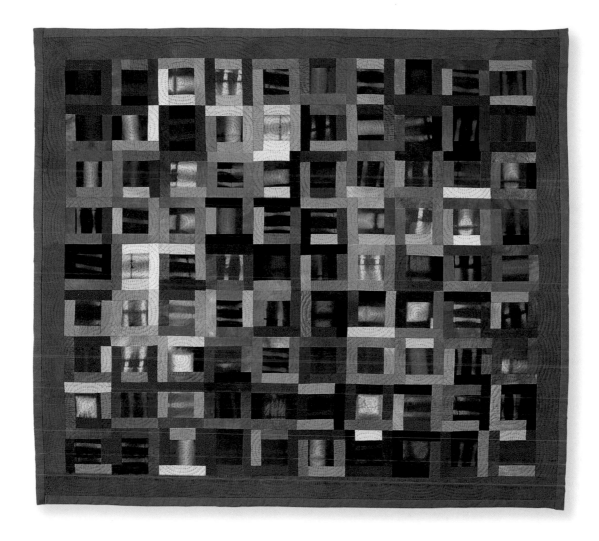

*Color Blocks #40*, ©1993. 49½" × 45". 100 percent cotton fabrics hand-dyed by Nancy Crow then resist-dyed by Lunn Fabrics. Fabrics cut Into directly and machine-pieced by Nancy Crow. Hand-quilted by Marie Moore with pattern denoted by Nancy Crow.

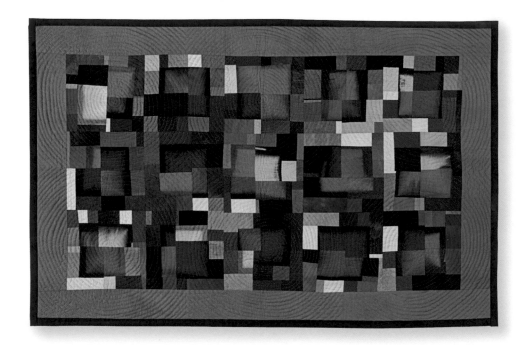

*Color Blocks #37*, ©1993. 43½" × 28½". 100 percent cotton fabrics hand-dyed by Nancy Crow then resist-dyed by Lunn Fabrics. Fabrics cut into directly and machine-pieced by Nancy Crow. Hand-quilted by Marla Hattabaugh with pattern denoted by Nancy Crow.

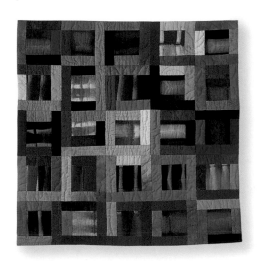

*Color Blocks #38*, ©1993. 23" × 23". 100 percent cotton fabrics hand-dyed by Nancy Crow then resist-dyed by Lunn Fabrics. Fabrics cut into directly and machine-pieced by Nancy Crow. Hand-quilted by Kris Doyle with pattern denoted by Nancy Crow.

*Color Blocks #39*, ©1993. 21" × 21". 100 percent cotton fabrics hand-dyed by Nancy Crow then resist-dyed by Lunn Fabrics. Fabrics cut into directly and machine-pieced by Nancy Crow. Hand-quilted by Kris Doyle with pattern denoted by Nancy Crow.

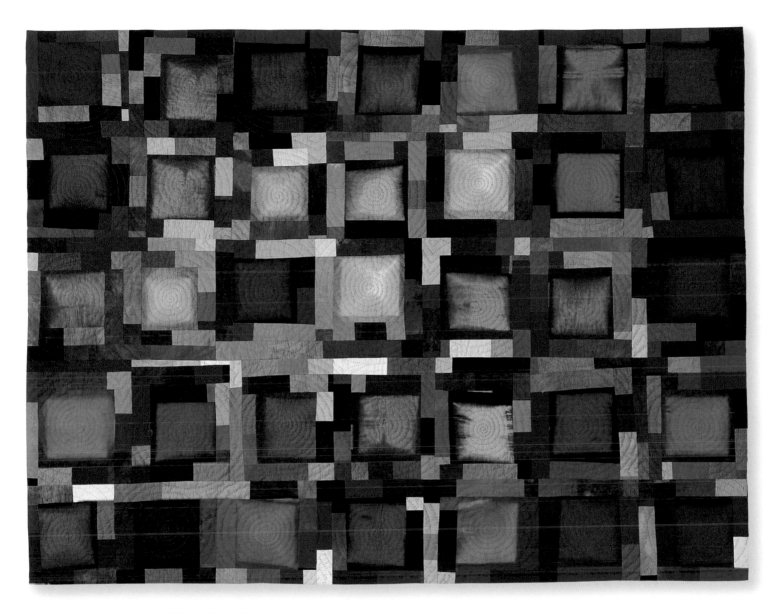

*Color Blocks #36*, ©1993.
58" × 45". 100 percent
cotton fabrics hand-dyed
by Nancy Crow then resist-
dyed by Lunn Fabrics.
Fabrics cut into directly
and machine-pieced
by Nancy Crow. Hand-
quilted by Marie Moore
with pattern denoted by
Nancy Crow.

**Color Blocks #41,**
©1993–1994. 51″ × 41″.
100 percent cotton fabrics
hand-dyed by Nancy Crow.
Fabrics cut into directly
and improvisationally;
machine-pieced by
Nancy Crow. Hand-quilted
by Marla Hattabaugh
with pattern denoted by
Nancy Crow.

**Color Blocks #42**, ©1994.
47″ × 31″. 100 percent
cotton fabrics hand-dyed
by Nancy Crow. Fabrics cut
into directly and machine-
pieced by Nancy Crow.
Hand-quilted by Kris Doyle
with pattern denoted by
Nancy Crow.

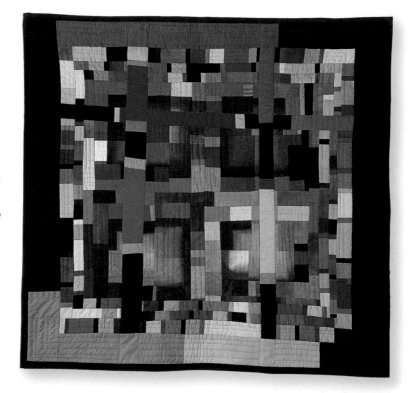

*Color Blocks #50*, ©1994.
35″ × 34¼″. 100 percent
cotton fabrics hand-dyed
by Nancy Crow. Fabrics cut
into directly and machine-
pieced by Nancy Crow.
Hand-quilted by Kris Doyle
with pattern denoted by
Nancy Crow.

*Color Blocks #51*, ©1994.
44″ × 42″. 100 percent
cotton fabrics hand-dyed
by Nancy Crow with center
square resist-dyed by
Lunn Fabrics. Fabrics cut
into directly and machine-
pieced by Nancy Crow.
Hand-quilted by Marie
Moore with pattern
denoted by Nancy Crow.

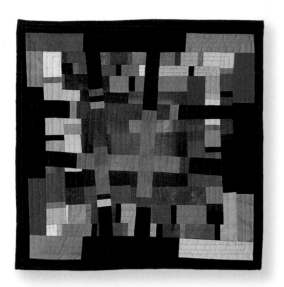

**Color Blocks #52**, ©1994.
22″ × 22″. 100 percent
cotton fabrics hand-dyed
by Nancy Crow with
squares resist-dyed by
Lunn Fabrics. Fabrics cut
into directly and machine-
pieced by Nancy Crow.
Hand-quilted by Marla
Hattabaugh with pattern
denoted by Nancy Crow.

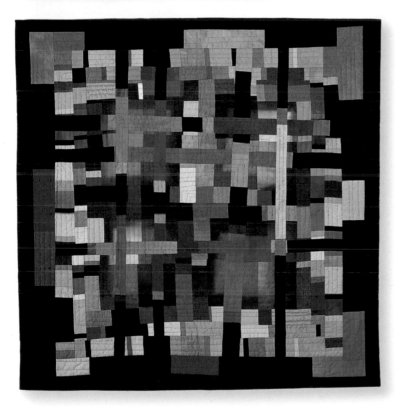

**Color Blocks #54**, ©1994.
32½″ × 33¼″. 100 percent
cotton fabrics hand-dyed
by Nancy Crow with
squares resist-dyed by
Lunn Fabrics. Fabrics cut
into directly and machine-
pieced by Nancy Crow.
Hand-quilted by Marla
Hattabaugh with pattern
denoted by Nancy Crow.

LEFT Color Blocks #51 *relates to* Color Blocks #75 *(see page 139)*. TOP Color Blocks #52, *a small quilt, is the study for* Color Blocks #56 *(see page 123).*

*Color Blocks #55*, ©1994.
41″ × 43″. 100 percent
cotton fabrics hand-dyed
by Nancy Crow. Fabrics cut
into directly and machine-
pieced by Nancy Crow.
Hand-quilted by Marla
Hattabaugh with pattern
denoted by Nancy Crow.

LEFT *Interior view of Studio #1 with hand-dyed fabrics.*

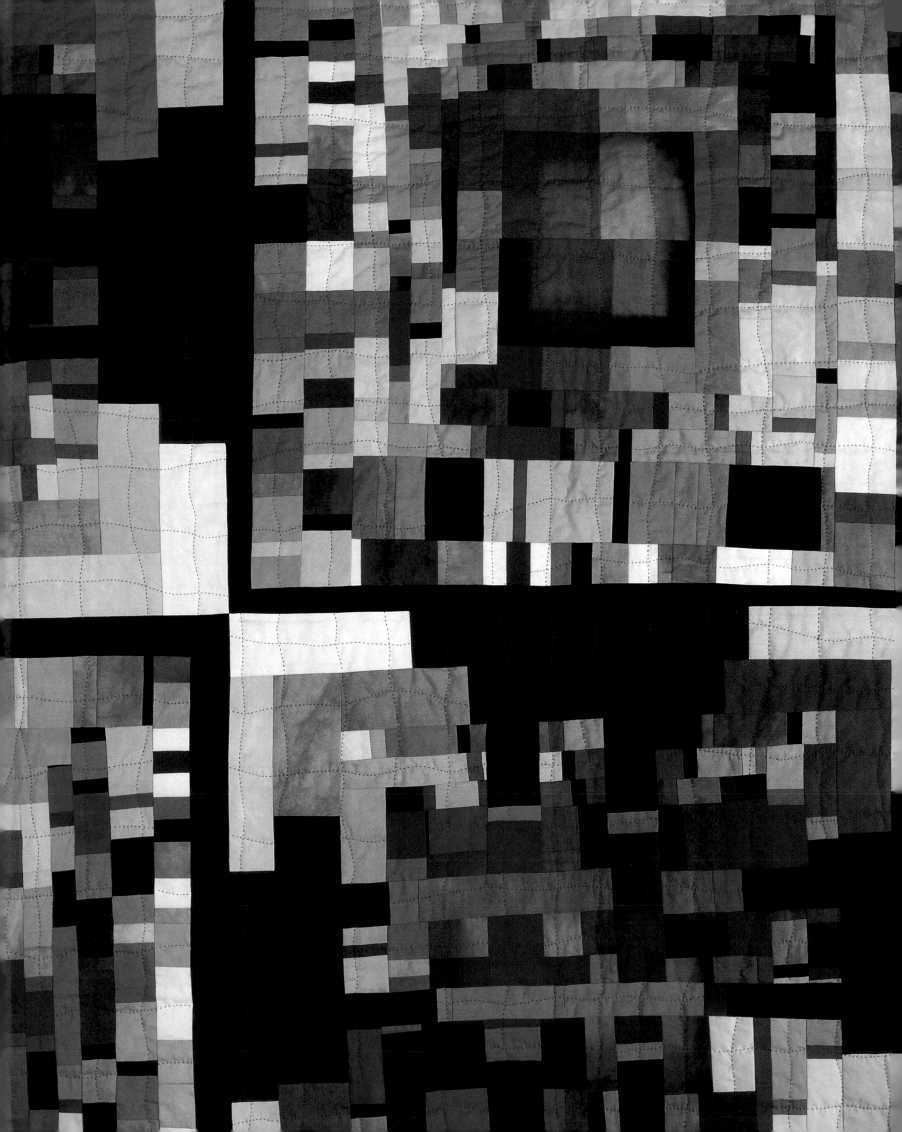

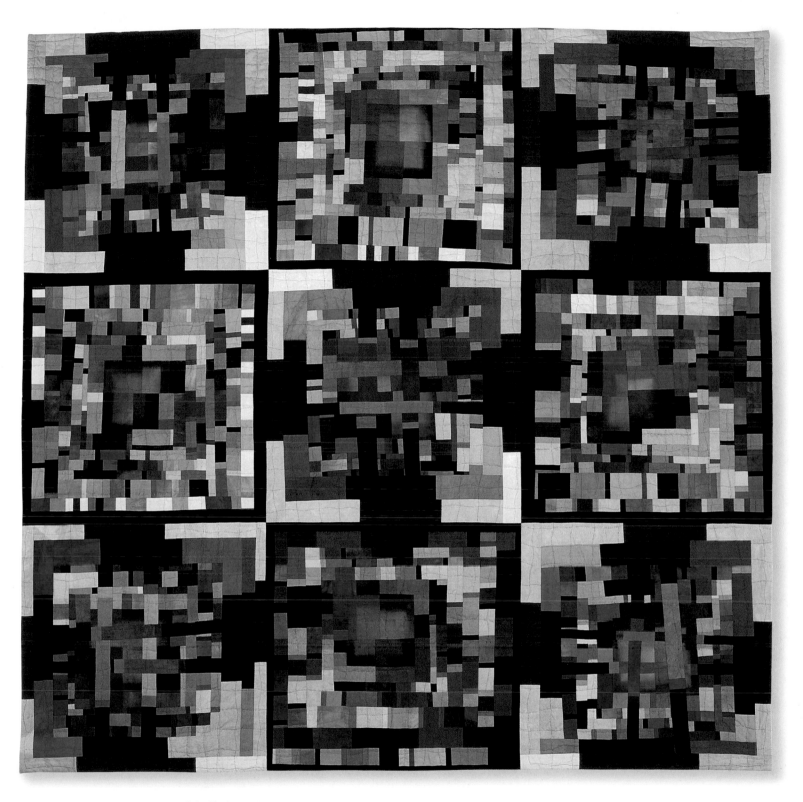

*Color Blocks #56*, ©1994.
69½″ × 70½″. 100 percent
cotton fabrics hand-dyed
by Nancy Crow with
squares resist-dyed by
Lunn Fabrics. Fabrics cut
into directly and machine-
pieced by Nancy Crow.
Hand-quilted by Marla
Hattabaugh with pattern
denoted by Nancy Crow.

***Color Blocks #57***, ©1994.
78″ × 69″. 100 percent
cotton fabrics hand-dyed
by Nancy Crow. Fabrics cut
into directly and machine-
pieced by Nancy Crow.
Hand-quilted by Marla
Hattabaugh with pattern
denoted by Nancy Crow.

ABOVE *Color Blocks #58 under construction in Studio #1 in December 1994. Although this quilt's orientation is vertical, I actually created it in sections on my big work wall, making more sections than I used. Because I was no longer able to climb up and down a ladder due to my painful knees, I figured out how to engineer the quilt working horizontally. I then pieced only five of the new sections together to create the vertical composition I wanted.*

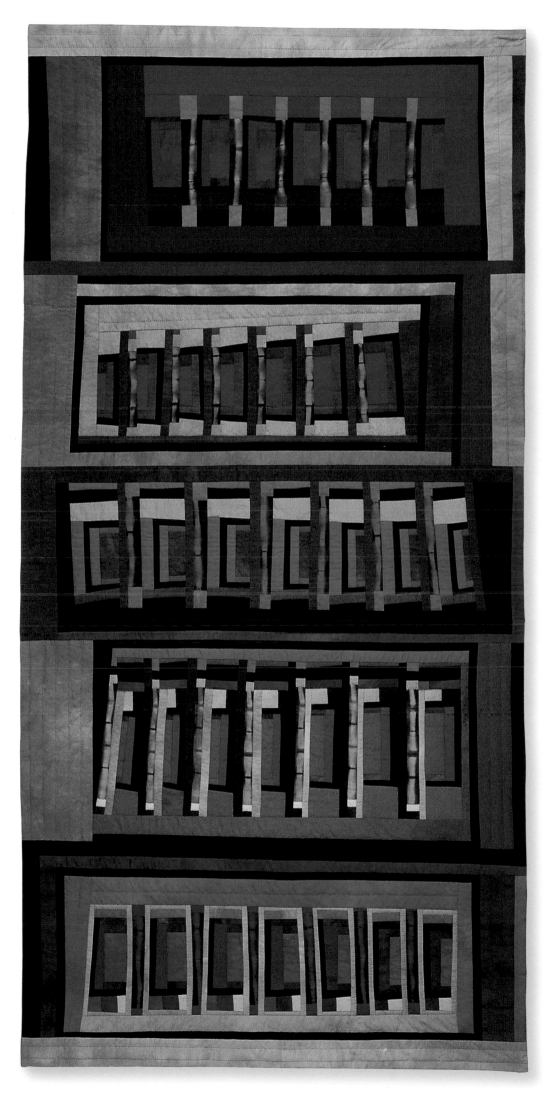

*Color Blocks #58*, ©1994.
41½″ × 88½″. 100 percent
cotton fabrics hand-dyed
by Nancy Crow with resist-
dyed fabrics by Lunn
Fabrics. Fabrics cut into
directly and machine-
pieced by Nancy Crow.
Hand-quilted by Marie
Moore with pattern
denoted by Nancy Crow.

*Color Blocks #59*, ©1994. 28½″ × 29½″. 100 percent cotton fabrics hand-dyed by Nancy Crow with squares resist-dyed by Lunn Fabrics. Fabrics cut into directly and machine-pieced by Nancy Crow. Hand-quilted by Marie Moore with pattern denoted by Nancy Crow.

*Color Blocks #60*, ©1994. 22½″ × 20¾″. 100 percent cotton fabrics hand-dyed by Nancy Crow with squares resist-dyed by Lunn Fabrics. Fabrics cut into directly and machine-pieced by Nancy Crow. Hand-quilted by Marie Moore with pattern denoted by Nancy Crow.

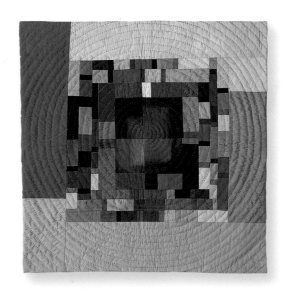

*Color Blocks #61*, ©1994. 22″ × 22½″. 100 percent cotton fabrics hand-dyed by Nancy Crow with squares resist-dyed by Lunn Fabrics. Fabrics cut into directly and machine-pieced by Nancy Crow. Hand-quilted by Marie Moore with pattern denoted by Nancy Crow.

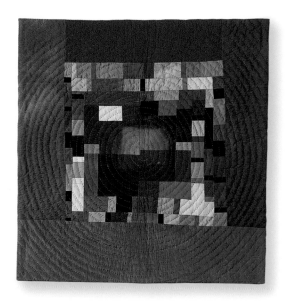

*Color Blocks #62*, ©1994.
22¾" × 24¼". 100 percent
cotton fabrics hand-dyed
by Nancy Crow with squares
resist-dyed by Lunn Fabrics.
Fabrics cut into directly
and machine-pieced by
Nancy Crow. Hand-quilted
by Marie Moore with pattern
denoted by Nancy Crow.

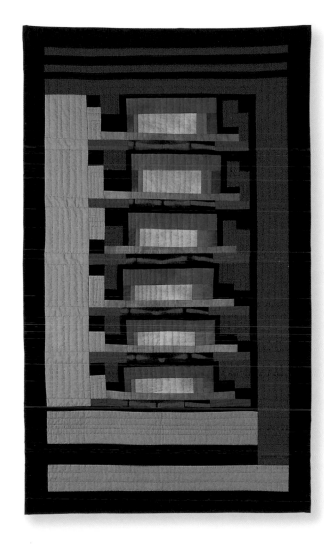

*Color Blocks #67*, ©1994.
26¼" × 44¾". 100 percent
cotton fabrics hand-dyed
by Nancy Crow with resist-
dyed fabrics by Lunn
Fabrics. Fabrics cut into
directly and machine-
pieced by Nancy Crow.
Hand-quilted by Kris Doyle
with pattern denoted by
Nancy Crow.

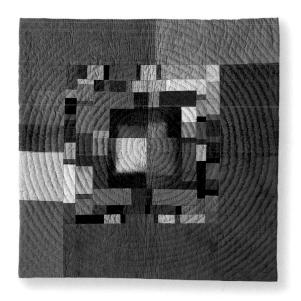

*Color Blocks #66*, ©1994.
23" × 23¼". 100 percent
cotton fabrics hand-dyed
by Nancy Crow with
squares resist-dyed by
Lunn Fabrics. Fabrics cut
into directly and machine-
pieced by Nancy Crow.
Hand-quilted by Marie
Moore with pattern
denoted by Nancy Crow.

ABOVE Color Blocks #69 *under construction in Studio #1 in June 1995.*

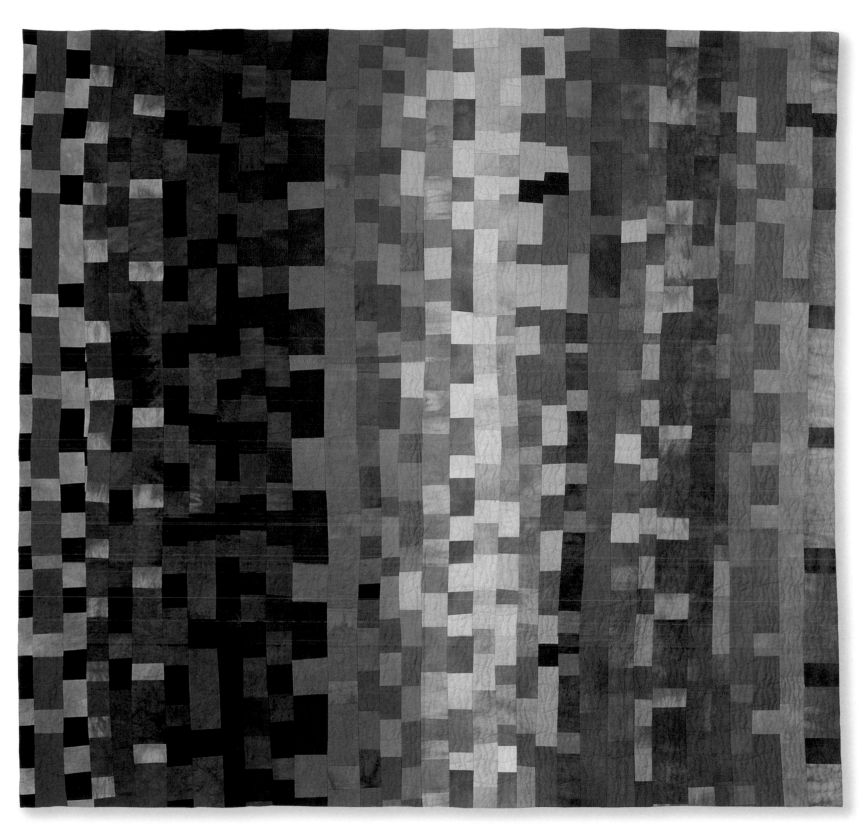

***Color Blocks #69***, ©1995.
85″ × 81½″. 100 percent
cotton fabrics hand-dyed
by Nancy Crow. Fabrics cut
into directly and machine-
pieced by Nancy Crow.
Hand-quilted by Marla
Hattabaugh with pattern
denoted by Nancy Crow.

ABOVE Color Blocks #70 *under construction in Studio #1 in July 1995. When I began work on* Color Blocks #70 *in July 1995 I knew I was in "search mode" once again. I wanted to become even freer in how I cut out shapes, in how I cut the edges of shapes and lines, in how I restructured the elements of my compositions.*

*Color Blocks #70*, ©1995.
64″ × 55″. 100 percent
cotton fabrics hand-dyed
by Nancy Crow. Fabrics cut
into directly and machine-
pieced by Nancy Crow.
Hand-quilted by Marla
Hattabaugh with pattern
denoted by Nancy Crow.

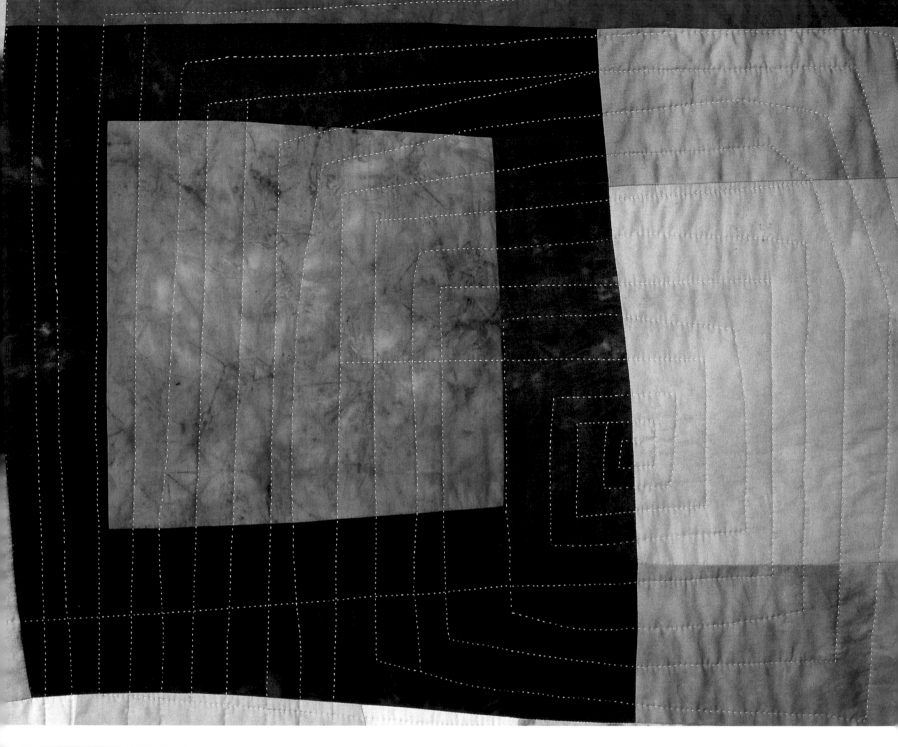

Color BLOCKS #71
( Mother, your
plaid house dresses
make me feel secure)
July 13, 1995)

QUILT TOP Pieced
July 6-9, 1995
out of my hand dyed
fabrics

Sent overnight to Sue Milling,
who received pkg. on July 10,
1995

ABOVE *With Color Blocks #71, I changed direction again, creating a much simpler composition. Not readily apparent is the raw emotion that drove this quilt. This was less than a year after I had seriously injured my knees and long before I underwent surgery (see pages 152–153). The pain in my knees was killing me. I recalled how bad my mother's knees became late in her life, and I remembered how stoic she was, never complaining about the pain to anyone. When I thought about this I realized what a profound lesson she had taught me. No one is interested in hearing about the pain. Everyone has problems. So I made this quilt as a loving gift to my mother. It is an exaggerated version of the plaids in the housedresses that had always comforted me to see her wear. Her housedresses meant she was getting down to business and focusing on the task at hand. I like to think that was one of the gifts she gave me—the ability to get started, get focused, and stay on task. This quilt relates to Color Blocks #42 (see page 117) and Constructions #15 (see page 192).* LEFT *Notes from my sketchbook.*

***Color Blocks #71***, ©1995.
56" × 66". 100 percent
cotton fabrics hand-dyed
by Nancy Crow. Fabrics cut
into directly and machine-
pieced by Nancy Crow.
Hand-quilted by Marla
Hattabaugh with pattern
denoted by Nancy Crow.

# SKETCHBOOK NOTES

▼ APRIL 18, 1995

My legs, my knees are causing me so much suffering, and I have gotten so little done, even started. My mind splinters as it tries and tries.

▼ FEBRUARY 3, 1996

Here it is, nearly 2:45 P.M., the sun out but SO COLD, nearly zero—actually 7°F. It seems I cannot focus. I clean off a shelf, dust my fabric off, refold some of it, and then restock the folds neatly back onto the shelf. I always pull out anything I no longer like and throw it into a growing pile of THINGS TO SELL. Then, instead of finishing this job, I am off trying to rearrange my office or paying bills or sitting watching birds or answering the phone or starting to clean the kitchen. Why am I fumbling around so? Because I am starting out again to make a new group of quilts. Studies first. But I can't seem to cut the first piece of fabric.

▼ FEBRUARY 8, 1996

Because I have too many ideas and willfully refuse to make myself STOP AND TRY JUST ONE IDEA. Internally, I want abundance, always abundance—or over-abundance, a sort of gasping for breath as the heart just pounds from over-stimulation. (My husband and I just had a short talk. He thinks nothing of walking into my studio to feed some tidbit into my brain—stopping my creative thoughts instantly. "Nancy, you need to call this person." "Don't forget to do that." "Do you remember what you agreed to do?" I said, please, please, we must come to an agreement that I have long periods undisturbed, please! I can't work with you constantly disturbing me! PLEASE!!!

LEFT *On September 19, 1996, almost one year after I had finished it, I decided* Color Blocks #72 *should be renamed* Constructions #1. *I was ready to begin a brand new series of work and this quilt embodied so many of the themes I wanted to explore.* RIGHT *I sold* Color Blocks #73 *and* Color Blocks #74 *as soon as I made them so I have no professionally photographed record of either . . . this was a mistake which I have tried to avoid since.*

## Color Blocks #72

Started at Arrowmont July 1995, while there teaching a 2-week class. I am not sure if it is some sort of break through. Actually did not work on it except July and September 12, 1995, when I finished it for Kris Doyle. 3 Day work?

Kris took it home Sept. 12, 1995, to quilt.

Renamed
Constructions #1
September 19, 1996

29" wide x 31/4" tall
finished size

Color BLOCKS #72
29½" X 32½" raw
July 26 – September 12, 1995
3rd version

Color BLOCKS #72
July 27 – September 12, 1995
2nd version

3/9/96 Color Blocks #73
manitoone

Color Blocks #73
June 1, 1996

Finished Size
14½" wide
X
20¾" tall

SOLD FOR $1800⁰⁰ at Studio B
in. No — Patti
made a mistake + sold it for $900 —
the wholesale price

$1700.

3/8/96 Color ³¹⁰ Blocks #74

Color Blocks #74
June 1, 1996

3/9/96 Color Blocks
marie moore

Small works made during
"Rest Period (thinking
period) between major
working months.
June 4, 1996

Always anxious about not
making more work! Actually
not pulling on all the ideas just
waiting.

(34) 1/13/97

winders off to other ideas of quilt to make.
Then I must grab it back — my focus, I must
grab it back, force it back to the piece, in this
case, CONSTRUCTIONS #4, that I am working
on this moment.

Yesterday and Saturday (Jan 11 and 12, 1997) I
decided to finish a piece I worked on last
year and perhaps back in 1991. Can't remember for
sure. Thank goodness I finished it yesterday as
I must get back to Constructions #4. The
quilt I finished is COLOR BLOCKS #75.

TOP

38" × 40" RAW

COLOR BLOCKS #75
Finished on Jan. 11-12, 1997
(Started center in 1991(?)

1/14/97 Dear Marla (copy of note)

BIG ONE ALMOST DONE.
In the meantime, please do a
bull's eye very close ½" to ⅓"
apart, irregular bull's eye.

I'm working hard! 1.6°F last
night! We love the fruit.
Nancy

*Color Blocks #75,*
©1996–1997. 38" × 40½".
100 percent cotton fabrics
hand-dyed by Nancy Crow
with center square resist-
dyed by Lunn Fabrics.
Fabrics cut into directly
and machine-pieced by
Nancy Crow. Hand-quilted
by Marla Hattabaugh
with pattern denoted by
Nancy Crow.

ABOVE Color Blocks #75 *relates to* Color Blocks #51 *(see page 118).*

LEFT *Notes from my sketchbooks.*

# LINEAR STUDIES

*Linear Study #1*, ©1993. 24″ × 24″. 100 percent cotton fabric hand-dyed by Nancy Crow with center square resist-dyed by Lunn Fabrics. Fabrics cut into directly and machine-pieced by Nancy Crow. Hand-quilted by Marla Hattabaugh with pattern denoted by Nancy Crow.

*In Linear Studies I wanted to draw lines with intent. I wanted to draw with a sharp blade and create an authentic edge along narrow widths of fabric. I am still learning.*

**Linear Study #2**, ©1994.
26″ × 26″. 100 percent
cotton fabric hand-dyed by
Nancy Crow  with center
square resist-dyed by
Lunn Fabrics. Fabrics cut
into directly and machine-
pieced by Nancy Crow.
Hand-quilted by Marla
Hattabaugh with pattern
denoted by Nancy Crow.

OPPOSITE, LEFT *Crab apple with five
branches forming parallel curves.*
OPPOSITE, RIGHT *Apple trees in early
spring. Notice the angular lines.*

# ARTIST'S STATEMENT

LINES. MY EYES FOLLOW lines with the fervor of addiction. Lines can push all my buttons, rush my senses into overload. Lines flood my mind with imagery . . . winds caressing branches or slamming them together . . . electric cables pulled and dumped into great swirls onto the pavement . . . dead brambles, fallen down, randomly overlapping one another . . . long, crooked branches, silent and graphic, elegant in the chill winter air . . . crab apple branches curving, creating a row of five pronounced parallel lines . . . narrow stems, so delicate, supporting their own shimmering flower heads . . . stands of grasses silently guarding the hills near the place where I grew up . . . cornstalks whispering to one another in our October fields.

Lines calm me down when they arrange themselves into rows, make patterns . . . make sense. Lines arouse anticipation when they swirl into energetic abstract elaborations. Lines become hypnotic when they are laid down in beautiful figure/ground relationships. Lines in nature form endless variations. Lines made by man do, too . . . but nature always wins!

I had always wanted to draw lines of my own in a masterful way; now I wanted to do so using a rotary cutter. To gain the control I needed, I had to practice cutting toward myself so that I could watch the edge of the razor-sharp blade as it sliced through the fabric. This became a form of drawing for me. My hand, wrist, arm, and shoulder muscles had to learn. They had to strengthen to draw well, and they had to cooperate with my eye. In *Linear Studies* I wanted to draw lines with intent. I wanted to draw with a sharp blade and create an authentic edge along narrow widths of fabric. I am still learning.

*Linear Study #3*,
©1994–1995. 49" × 57".
100 percent cotton
fabric hand-dyed by
Nancy Crow. Fabrics cut
into directly and machine-
pieced by Nancy Crow.
Hand-quilted by Marla
Hattabaugh with pattern
denoted by Nancy Crow.

PHOTOS 1 AND 2 *Grasses silently guard the hills near my childhood home.* PHOTO 3 *Curvilinear branches of a bush.* PHOTO 4 *Burned out electric cable, thrown onto pavement.*

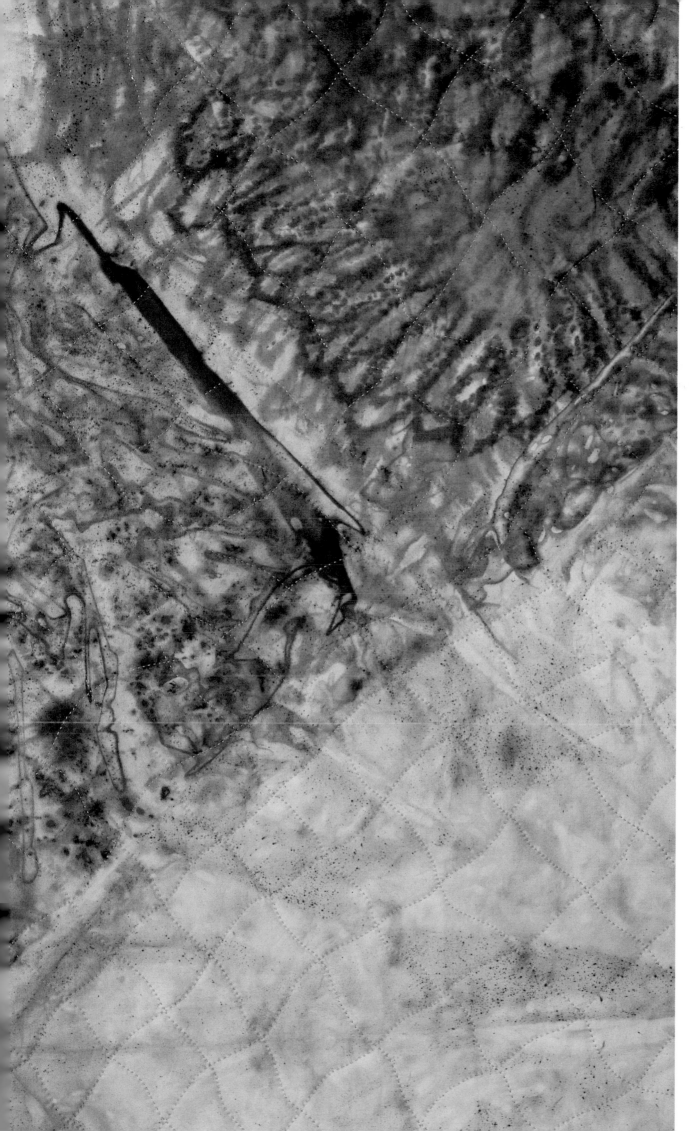

1

2

3

4

# SKETCHBOOK NOTES

▼ JANUARY 7, 1995

This morning, everyone in this household is in such a bad mood. I love
the quietness and spirituality of my studio—a world to escape to. It seems
we are all trying to do far more than is possible, and we get grumpy.
I have to clean the second studio so that Kevin can do photography
tomorrow. I have saved so many cardboard boxes. I hate to burn them,
but they are filling up the room.

PHOTO 1 *Dried stalks.* PHOTO 2 *Lines of stems.* PHOTO 3 *Poison ivy twines up a telephone pole.*
PHOTO 4 *Stalks of field corn.* PHOTO 5 *Dried stems.*

*Linear Study #4*, ©1995.
15¾″ × 53½″. 100 percent
cotton fabric hand-dyed
by Nancy Crow. Fabrics cut
into directly and machine-
pieced by Nancy Crow.
Hand-quilted by Marla
Hattabaugh with pattern
denoted by Nancy Crow.

*Linear Study #5*, ©1995. 18″ × 47″. 100 percent cotton fabric hand-dyed by Nancy Crow with center square resist-dyed by Lunn Fabrics. Fabrics cut into directly and machine-pieced by Nancy Crow. Hand-quilted by Kris Doyle with pattern denoted by Nancy Crow.

*Linear Study #6*, ©1995.
24″ × 61″. 100 percent
cotton fabric hand-dyed
by Nancy Crow. Fabrics cut
into directly and machine-
pieced by Nancy Crow.
Hand-quilted by Marla
Hattabaugh with pattern
denoted by Nancy Crow.

*Linear Study #7*, ©1995.
39" × 42". 100 percent
cotton fabric hand-dyed
by Nancy Crow with center
square resist-dyed by
Lunn Fabrics. Fabrics cut
into directly and machine-
pieced by Nancy Crow.
Hand-quilted by Marla
Hattabaugh with pattern
denoted by Nancy Crow.

# LINEAR STUDIES IN MONOCHROME

I ALWAYS ASK MY PHOTOGRAPHER, J. Kevin Fitzsimons, to take black-and-white photos of each completed quilt using a 2¼" format. These photographs enable me to have a record of how successfully I used value in each composition.

Linear Study #1

Linear Study #2

Linear Study #3

Linear Study #4

Linear Study #7

Linear Study #9

Linear Study #10

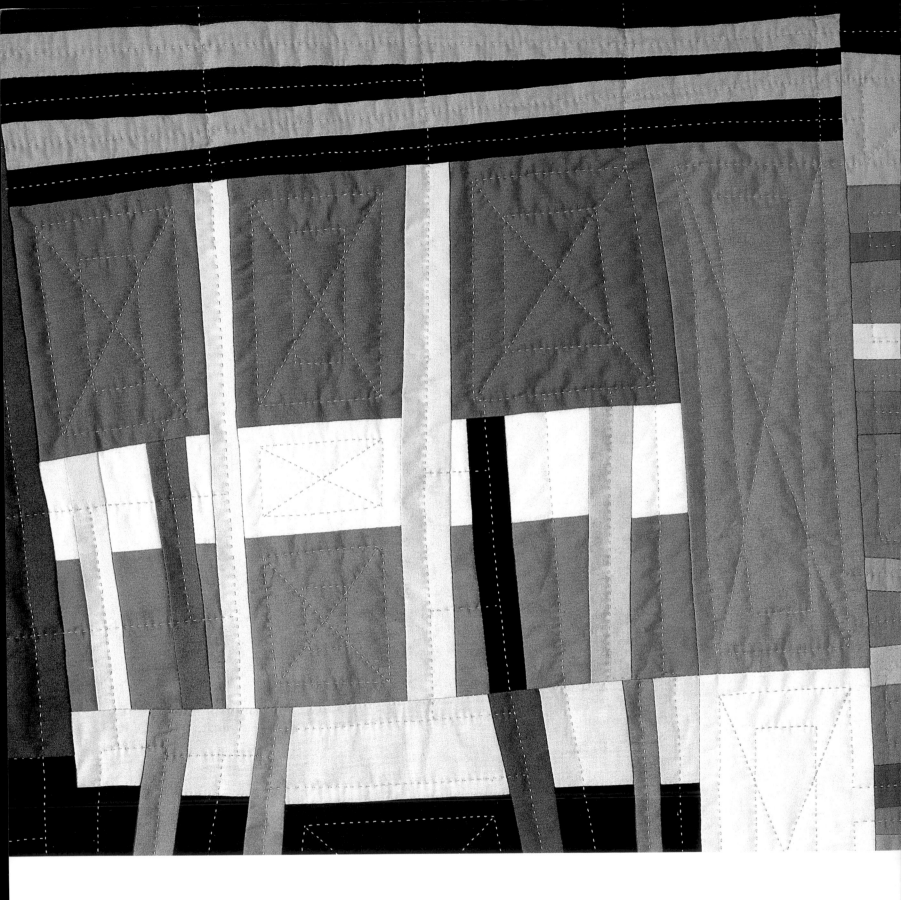

Linear Study #8 *was an aberration. It is quite different from the other works in the series for a reason. When I began working on this quilt in 1995, I was struggling with severe, ongoing pain in both my knees. It began late in 1994 after I crashed into our concrete steps while dashing out of my studio to check a pot I had left cooking on the kitchen stove. This was the fourth time I had gone down so hard on my knees. I knew I was in trouble. My knees swelled, turned black and blue, and began to ache. They ached without let-up for the next five years. From that point on, I became fixated on controlling the pain. I would not give up quiltmaking even though it involved so much standing. As I worked on Linear Study #8 the pain became so intense that I had to strap the fronts of both knees to keep the pain under control and*

*Linear Study #8*, ©1995. 40½″ × 45″. 100 percent cotton fabric hand-dyed by Nancy Crow. Fabrics cut into directly and machine-pieced by Nancy Crow. Hand-quilted by Marla Hattabaugh with pattern denoted by Nancy Crow.

*to prevent my legs from bowing further outwards. When I finished, I knew that this quilt was about my knees and the pain I was experiencing. I finally underwent knee-replacement surgery for the left knee in 1998. Frightened at the prospect of another operation, I waited until 2000 to have the right knee joint replaced. As a consequence of waiting, my right knee deteriorated and required more extensive surgery. Today, I am a new person . . . full of life and energy, with none of my thoughts or emotions caught in a stranglehold over pain control. Pain impacted all of my work from 1995 to 2000, but it is particularly evident in* Linear Study #8. *The approach I took in this quilt was used again in* Constructions #18 *and I hope to explore it further in the future.*

*Linear Study #9*, ©1995. 44″ × 56½″. 100 percent cotton fabric hand-dyed by Nancy Crow with center square resist-dyed by Lunn Fabrics. Fabrics cut into directly and machine-pieced by Nancy Crow. Hand-quilted by Marla Hattabaugh with pattern denoted by Nancy Crow.

**Linear Study #10**, ©1995.
30½″ × 30½″. 100 percent
cotton fabric hand-dyed
by Nancy Crow with center
square resist-dyed by
Lunn Fabrics. Fabrics cut
into directly and machine-
pieced by Nancy Crow.
Hand-quilted by Marla
Hattabaugh with pattern
denoted by Nancy Crow.

# CONSTRUCTIONS

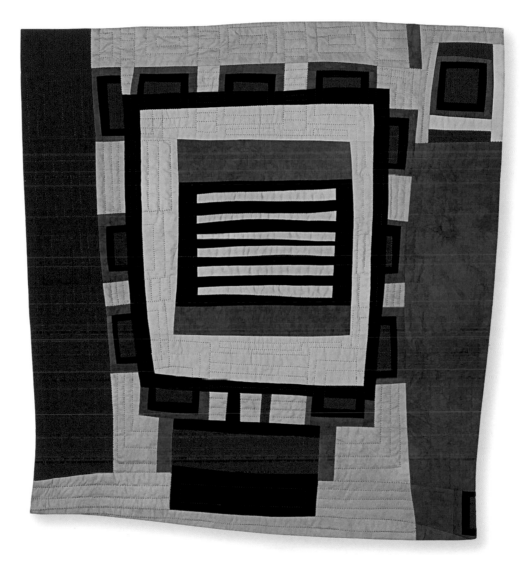

*Constructions #1*, ©1995.
28½″ × 30¾″. 100 percent
cotton fabrics hand-dyed
by Nancy Crow. Fabrics
cut and machine-pieced
improvisationally by
Nancy Crow. Hand-quilted
by Marla Hattabaugh
with pattern denoted by
Nancy Crow.

DECEMBER 17 TO 18, 2004 | SKETCHBOOK NOTES

*Here we go in earnest! I will give my soul and mind and all that is far, far inside both (that mysterious place that shelters surprise) to the direction the fabrics and colors and shapes lead me in understanding.*

# ARTIST'S STATEMENT

I LIKE CONSTRUCTIONS—pieces and parts of shapes and lines somehow fitting together. I admire all types of constructions: well-designed buildings, beautiful roof lines, Chinese roof tiles made of clay, timber-frame barns, thick walls of old brick, small panes of glass encased by wooden mullions, huge elaborate porches, fancy gingerbread trims, massive stone foundations, and intricate trellises. As a child, I screamed with frustration every time my brother dragged out our large cardboard box of Lincoln Logs. I hated those boring brown logs, all the same color, all similar shapes! Anything I ever built fell apart. They were BORING. Even so, they somehow managed to affect me, because NOW, TODAY I know that I MUST, that I NEED to put my fabric shapes together as constructions, as though they are wooden pieces that fit together. My shapes must be exaggerated and lyrical. And they must be cut spontaneously out of limitless colors. Where shapes join together, something miraculous might transpire there, too!

And so, in the hot summer of 1995, I commenced to cut out and sew together *Constructions #1*. At the time, I was teaching a two-week workshop at The Arrowmont School of Arts and Crafts in Gatlinburg, Tennessee. After lunch, I gave my students a timed five-hour design exercise, only to hear them erupt into complaints that it was too hard to do so much in such a short time. I rose to the challenge, telling them I would work alongside them and create a finished composition, too. I would cut out fabrics and sew my composition together during the time allowed to prove that it could be done. My ideas flowed. I stayed focused. I proceeded to create the composition, *Constructions #1*, that would contain nearly every theme that has absorbed me since.

Working on the *Constructions* series has honed my eye to ever more dynamic proportions: shape to shape, line to line, space to space, color to color, and value to value. In future work, I hope the word "exquisitely" will become fast partners with the word "dynamic," as I work with proportions. I also hope that my own internal and mysterious rhythms will be revealed by a body of work that to my standards is thoroughly honest.

*The interior of Studio #1, taken on July 18, 2005, showing the north work wall.*

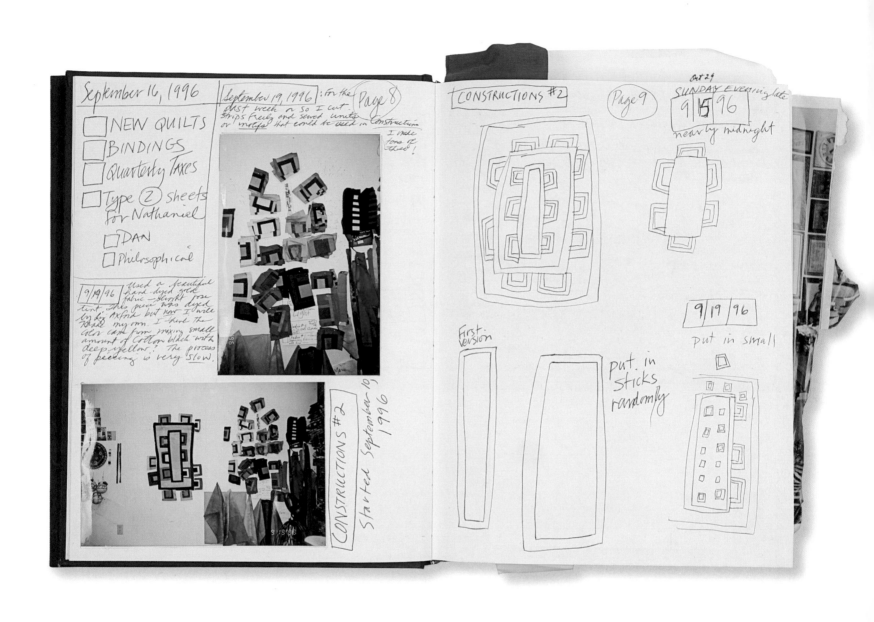

*I began making parts for my Constructions in early September, 1996, although I did not make note of the exact day. I had returned from South Africa on August 5, 1996, and it seemed very difficult to RE-ENTER the shelter of my studio as I felt I had changed somehow or at least had been so affected by my stay in South Africa that I KNEW I WANTED TO CHANGE. So at first I had to re-order my studio by restacking my fabrics, cleaning the large walls, and putting up new items to inspire me. I rolled out the long raffia appliqué dance skirt I had purchased in Capetown (it was from the Kuba kingdom, Kasai region, Democratic Republic of Congo, formerly Zaire). Matthew climbed a ladder to pin it high on the wall. As usual I pinned many, many ideas along the lower part of the wall so I could stare at these "beginnings" and see if any inspired me to go on. In the center I pinned Constructions #1 (yellow, blue, red) which I made at Arrowmont in July 1995. I gave myself the challenge of making a study in five hours or at least in part of one day. Wish I had kept notes. If I can release to a non-critical state, I can flow and ideas come rapidly.*

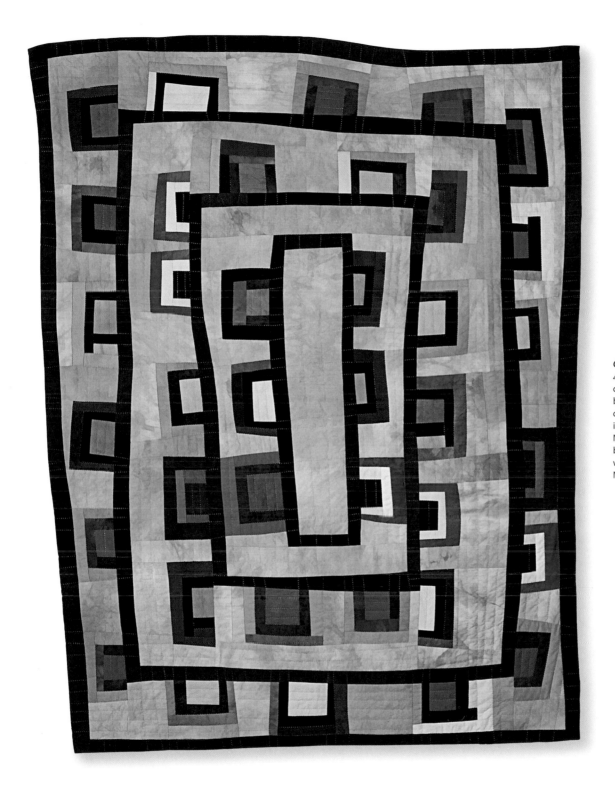

*Constructions #2*, ©1996. 40″ × 51″. 100 percent cotton fabrics hand-dyed by Nancy Crow. Fabrics cut and machine-pieced improvisationally by Nancy Crow. Hand-quilted by Marla Hattabaugh with pattern denoted by Nancy Crow.

*Constructions #3*, ©1997.
34″ × 49″. 100 percent
cotton fabrics hand-dyed
by Nancy Crow. Fabrics
cut and machine-pieced
improvisationally by
Nancy Crow. Hand-quilted
by Marla Hattabaugh
with pattern denoted by
Nancy Crow.

ABOVE *A large sketchbook with a photo of Constructions #1 glued inside, along with other sketchbooks on my large worktable in Studio #1.* RIGHT *Sketchbooks on my work table.*

# FROM SKETCHES TO *CONSTRUCTIONS*

I, LIKE MOST SERIOUS ARTISTS, have my own unique and specific ways of gathering ideas that result in compositions. Often, a particular visual incident (walking around our fields, staring out the window at trees, going through books of photos) floods my brain with images that instantly translate into configurations that are complete compositions right at that moment. The images are always geometric shapes or lines that I could cut easily out of my fabrics. But if I do not record a composition at that moment, it is usually lost or becomes part of another, similar visual incident.

I know I should carry my sketchbook with me constantly, but I am not in the habit of doing so because the large 9" by 12" sketchbooks I prefer are quite heavy and cumbersome. Instead, I often draw compositional ideas on small pieces of heavy paper that I carry in my purse along with my drawing pens. These are nothing more than odds and ends of cardstock. I eventually glue these cursory drawings down in my sketchbook with a date and comments. As I spread my sketchbooks out on tables, I feel exhilarated at the abundance of ideas and possibilities they contain. I want to start working. But, at this point, I always start grappling with FOCUS—getting focused, staying focused, and remaining on task. Sometimes I have wondered if the truly great artists who have accomplished so much in their lifetimes simply did not have this ongoing struggle. This question has always perplexed me. But I know that once I find a pathway to focus, I stay disciplined. The work pours out even though the initial struggle is always with my brain as it scrambles in every direction, flailing at one idea after another, after another, searching for the "best" idea, until I allow myself to become totally overwhelmed and exhausted! I ask myself what this behavior is all about. Is it procrastination? Over-stimulation? Lack of control?

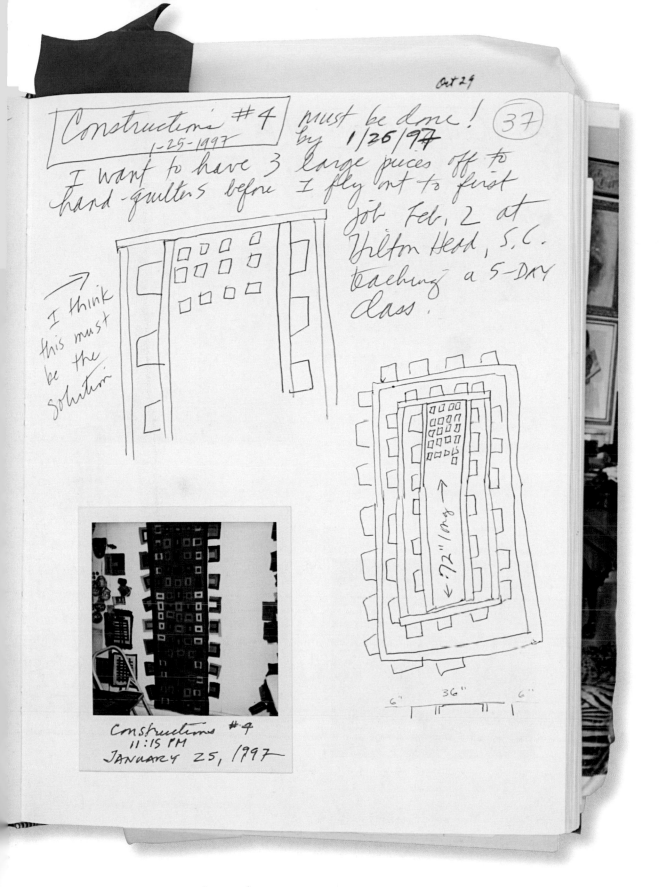

*Oct 29*

Constructions #4
1-25-1997
must be done! (37)
by 1/26/97

I want to have 3 large pieces off to hand-quilters before I fly out to first job Feb. 2 at Hilton Head, S.C. teaching a 5-DAY class.

I think this must be the solution →

← 72"/ong →

6"  36"  6"

Constructions #4
11:15 PM
JANUARY 25, 1997

Constructions #4. I am working on the center of this "large" quilt. I am not sure the top row is "working." That is, perhaps it is just "extra," making the composition cluttered and not clear. I may yet take off the top row but will wait till I have worked in the rest of the rows. DOUBTS? My doubts, if any, rear their head by saying—is this piece TOO simple? Is it dynamic? Why am I making it? BUT I AM MAKING IT BECAUSE IT COMES OUT ON ITS OWN.
I need to make my own nomad rugs, rugs that symbolize my solitude, my lifestyle of being alone on this farm, of trying to understand what my life is about. My nomad rugs . . . these first constructions. All of my piecing of fabrics reflects strong needs. I feel WHOLE when I work in my studio. CONTINUES ON JANUARY 13 There I am happy—usually totally absorbed in thoughts. Always struggling to stay focused because my mind just goes and goes and goes in such scattered directions. Ideas flooding on top of flooding ideas. My attention wanders off to other ideas of quilts to make. Then I must grab it back—my focus. I must grab it back, force it back to the piece, in this case, Constructions #4.

*Constructions #4,*
©1996–1997. 38½" × 91".
100 percent cotton fabrics
hand-dyed by Nancy Crow.
Fabrics cut and machine-
pieced improvisationally by
Nancy Crow. Hand-quilted
by Marla Hattabaugh
with pattern denoted by
Nancy Crow.

*The start of* Constructions #5 *on my work wall in Studio #1.*

*Constructions #5*, ©1997.
34¼″ × 58″. 100 percent
cotton fabrics hand-dyed
by Nancy Crow. Fabrics
cut and machine-pieced
improvisationally by
Nancy Crow. Hand-quilted
by Marla Hattabaugh
with pattern denoted by
Nancy Crow.

Hand-made clay
and straw bricks in
Chiapas, Mexico.

*Constructions #6*, ©1997.
26″ × 34″. 100 percent
cotton fabrics hand-dyed
by Nancy Crow. Fabrics
cut and machine-pieced
improvisationally by
Nancy Crow. Hand-quilted
by Kris Doyle with pattern
denoted by Nancy Crow.

*Squares on one of the monuments in the main cemetery, Chichicastenango, Guatemala. These monuments were very important and powerful images for me when working on the Constructions series.*

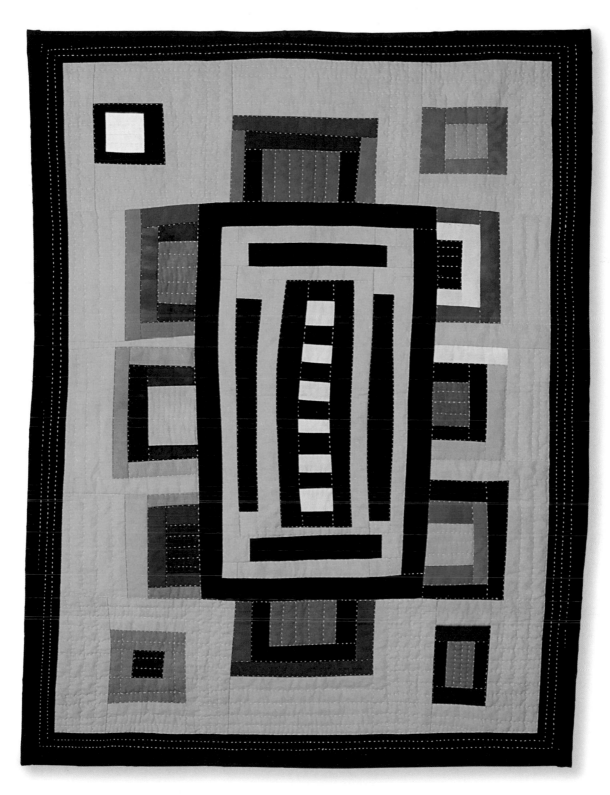

*Constructions #6A*, ©1997.
23" × 30". 100 percent
cotton fabrics hand-dyed
by Nancy Crow. Fabrics
cut and machine-pieced
improvisationally by
Nancy Crow. Hand-
quilted by Marie Moore
with pattern denoted by
Nancy Crow.

*Constructions #7*, ©1997. 49″ × 69″. 100 percent cotton fabrics hand-dyed by Nancy Crow. Fabrics cut and machine-pieced improvisationally by Nancy Crow. Hand-quilted by Marla Hattabaugh with pattern denoted by Nancy Crow.

Finely woven Mexican baskets on top of my hand-dyed cottons in Studio #1. The patterns on these baskets inspired aspects of the entire Constructions series.

***Constructions #8***, ©1997. 38¼″ × 40½″. 100 percent cotton fabrics hand-dyed by Nancy Crow. Fabrics cut and machine-pieced improvisationally by Nancy Crow. Hand-quilted by Lou DeLay with pattern denoted by Nancy Crow.

*The south wall of Crow Timber Frame Barn as it was being renovated. I relate this image to the composition of* Constructions #8.

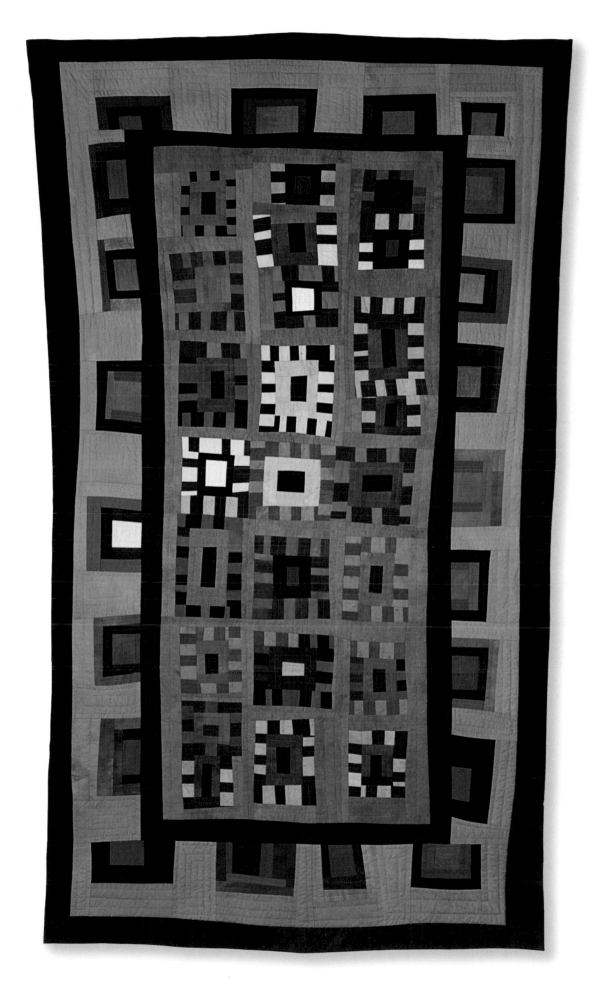

*Constructions #9*, ©1997.
40" × 72". 100 percent
cotton fabrics hand-dyed
by Nancy Crow. Fabrics
cut and machine-pieced
improvisationally by
Nancy Crow. Hand-quilted
by Marla Hattabaugh
with pattern denoted by
Nancy Crow.

*This 1800s antique quilt was hand-pieced from wool and silk, with the initials G.C. embroidered in the large center square. I bought this quilt because I loved the composition of squares. Another compelling reason for buying this quilt was that the initials are the same of those of my father, Glenn Crow, and I wondered if perhaps his mother could have made it.*

*Constructions #10*, ©1997.
31″ × 81″. 100 percent
cotton fabrics hand-dyed
by Nancy Crow. Fabrics
cut and machine-pieced
improvisationally by
Nancy Crow. Hand-quilted
by Marla Hattabaugh
with pattern denoted by
Nancy Crow.

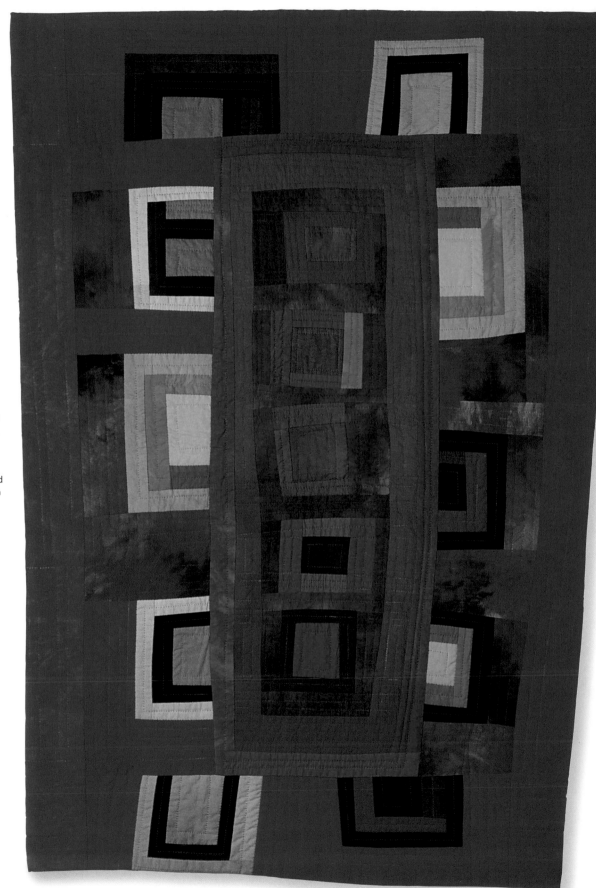

*Constructions #11*, ©1997. 25½″ × 39¼″. 100 percent cotton fabrics hand-dyed by Nancy Crow. Fabrics cut and machine-pieced improvisationally by Nancy Crow. Hand-quilted by Lou Delay with pattern denoted by Nancy Crow.

*Constructions #13*, ©1997. 18¼″ × 31¼″. 100 percent cotton fabrics hand-dyed by Nancy Crow. Fabrics cut and machine-pieced improvisationally by Nancy Crow. Hand-quilted by Marla Hattabaugh with pattern denoted by Nancy Crow.

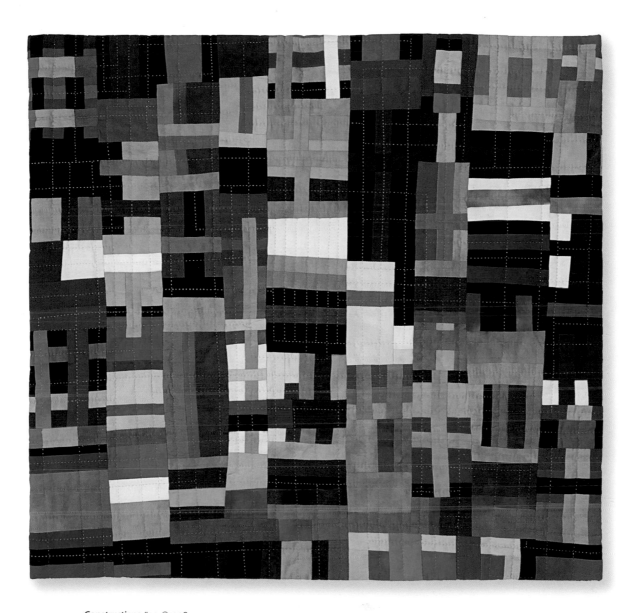

**Constructions #14**, ©1998.
24″ × 23″. 100 percent
cotton fabrics hand-dyed
by Nancy Crow. Fabrics
cut and machine-pieced
improvisationally by
Nancy Crow. Hand-quilted
by Marla Hattabaugh
with pattern denoted by
Nancy Crow.

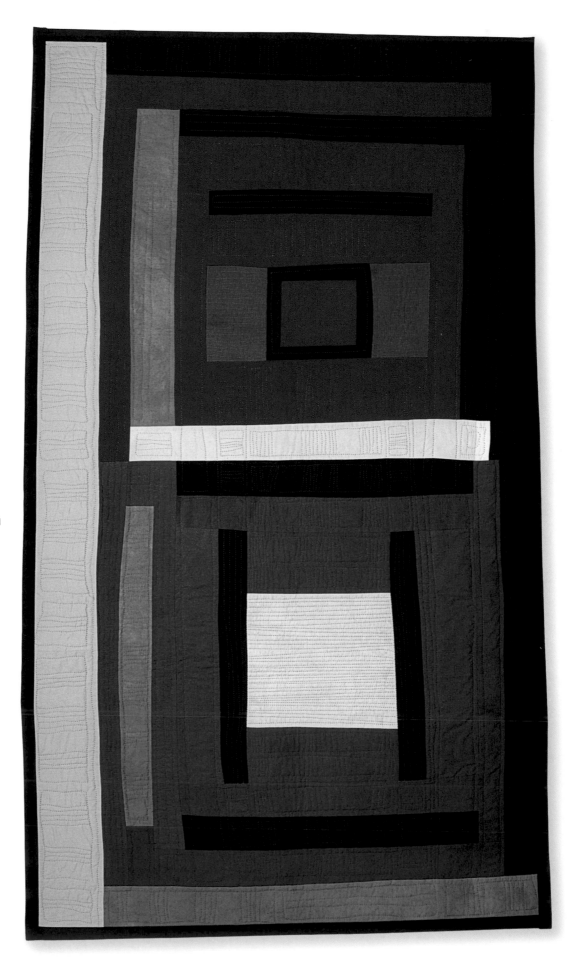

*Constructions #15*, ©1998.
34½″ × 64″. 100 percent
cotton fabrics hand-dyed
by Nancy Crow. Fabrics
cut and machine-pieced
improvisationally by
Nancy Crow. Hand-quilted
by Marla Hattabaugh
with pattern denoted by
Nancy Crow.

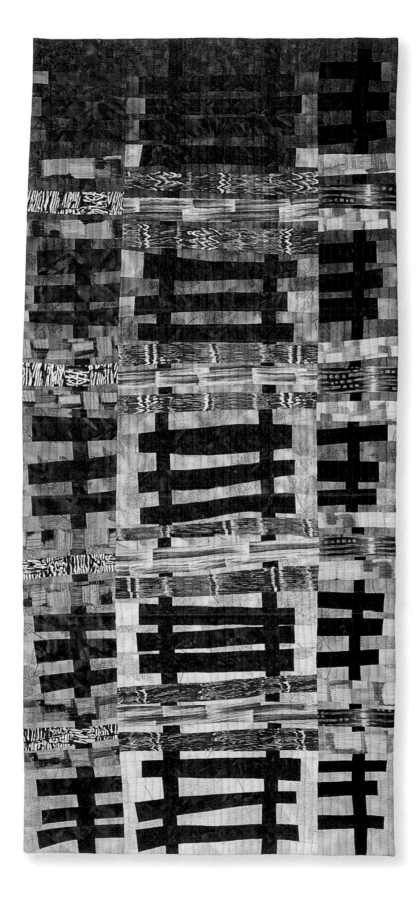

*Constructions #16*, ©1998. 24½" × 54". 100 percent cotton fabrics hand-dyed by Nancy Crow. Fabrics cut and machine-pieced improvisationally by Nancy Crow. Hand-quilted by Marla Hattabaugh with pattern denoted by Nancy Crow.

*When I started this piece (Constructions #17) I was reacting to my aversion to working with prints. I needed clean lines and pure clean colors, not textured prints. I had already sewn lots of strips together, selvage to selvage, the previous August while teaching for two weeks at Arrowmont. I brought back stacks of sewn-together strips around 12" across by 44" long. The stacks had been sitting on the floor beneath and behind my cutting table. Every now and then I would look at them when I was behind the table, pinning on the wall. So while working on Constructions #16, I began picking up the stripped fabrics and studying them, and then quickly pinned up an arrangement I liked IMMEDIATELY. When I started on this piece I pinned it correctly onto my work wall on west side and started using my small step ladder. Though the quilt top looks like it might be simple to do, it was actually quite difficult to sew together. Constant getting up and down my ladder to cut and re-cut and sew.*

*Constructions #17*, ©1998. 41″ × 82″. 100 percent cotton fabrics hand-dyed by Nancy Crow. Fabrics cut and machine-pieced improvisationally by Nancy Crow. Hand-quilted by Marla Hattabaugh with pattern denoted by Nancy Crow.

1

2

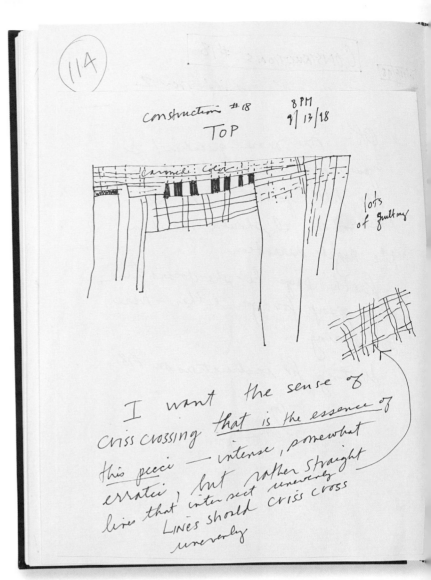

114

Construction #18     8 PM
                     9/13/18
TOP

Caramel: Color

lots
of quilting

I want the sense of
criss crossing that is the essence of
this piece — intense, somewhat
erratic but rather straight
lines that intersect unevenly.
LINES should criss cross
unevenly

3

4

*Constructions #18*, ©1998.
42″ × 37″. 100 percent
cotton fabrics hand-dyed
by Nancy Crow. Fabrics
cut and machine-pieced
improvisationally by
Nancy Crow. Hand-quilted
by Marla Hattabaugh
with pattern denoted by
Nancy Crow.

PHOTOS 1 AND 2 *Debris from a building as it is torn down.* PHOTO 3 *Drawings
from my sketchbook.* PHOTO 4 *This image relates to the feeling I was trying for
in* Constructions #18.

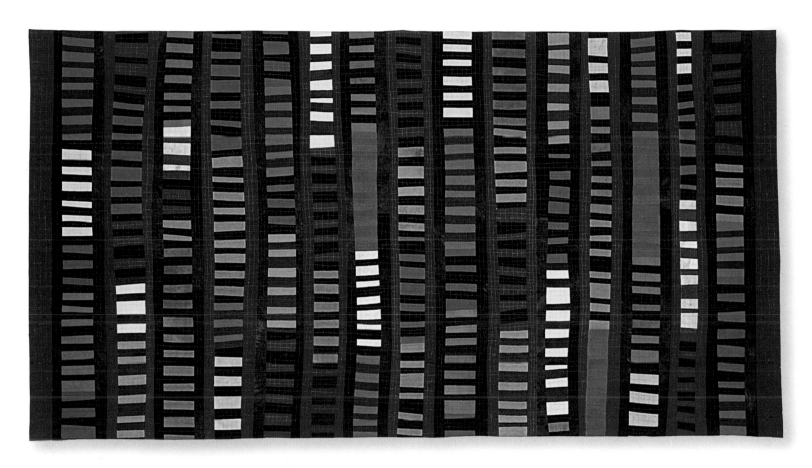

*Constructions #21*, ©1999.
73″ × 40″. 100 percent
cotton fabrics hand-dyed
by Nancy Crow. Fabrics
cut and machine-pieced
improvisationally by
Nancy Crow. Hand-quilted
by Marla Hattabaugh
with pattern denoted by
Nancy Crow.

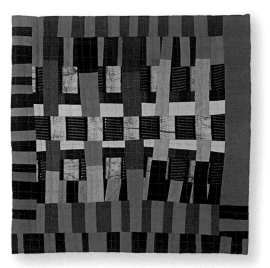

*Constructions #22*, ©1999. 15½″ × 15½″. 100 percent cotton fabrics hand-dyed by Nancy Crow. Fabrics cut and machine-pieced improvisationally by Nancy Crow. Hand-quilted by Marla Hattabaugh with pattern denoted by Nancy Crow.

*Constructions #23*, ©1999. 11¾″ × 10¾″. 100 percent cotton fabrics hand-dyed by Nancy Crow. Fabrics cut and machine-pieced improvisationally by Nancy Crow. Hand-quilted by Marla Hattabaugh with pattern denoted by Nancy Crow.

*Constructions #24*, ©1999. 18″ × 37″. 100 percent cotton fabrics hand-dyed by Nancy Crow. Fabrics cut and machine-pieced improvisationally by Nancy Crow. Hand-quilted by Marla Hattabaugh with pattern denoted by Nancy Crow.

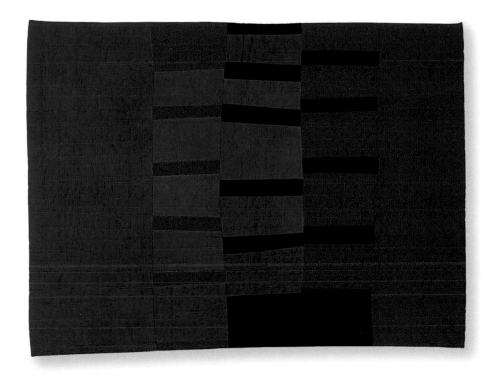

*Constructions #25*, ©1999. 27½″ × 20½″. 100 percent cotton fabrics hand-dyed by Nancy Crow. Fabrics cut and machine-pieced improvisationally by Nancy Crow. Hand-quilted by Marla Hattabaugh with pattern denoted by Nancy Crow.

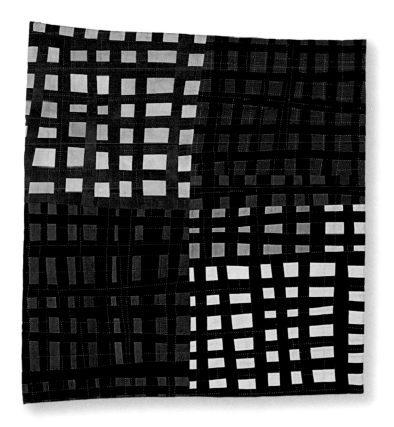

*Constructions #26*, ©1999. 24″ × 25½″. 100 percent cotton fabrics hand-dyed by Nancy Crow. Fabrics cut and machine-pieced improvisationally by Nancy Crow. Hand-quilted by Marla Hattabaugh with pattern denoted by Nancy Crow.

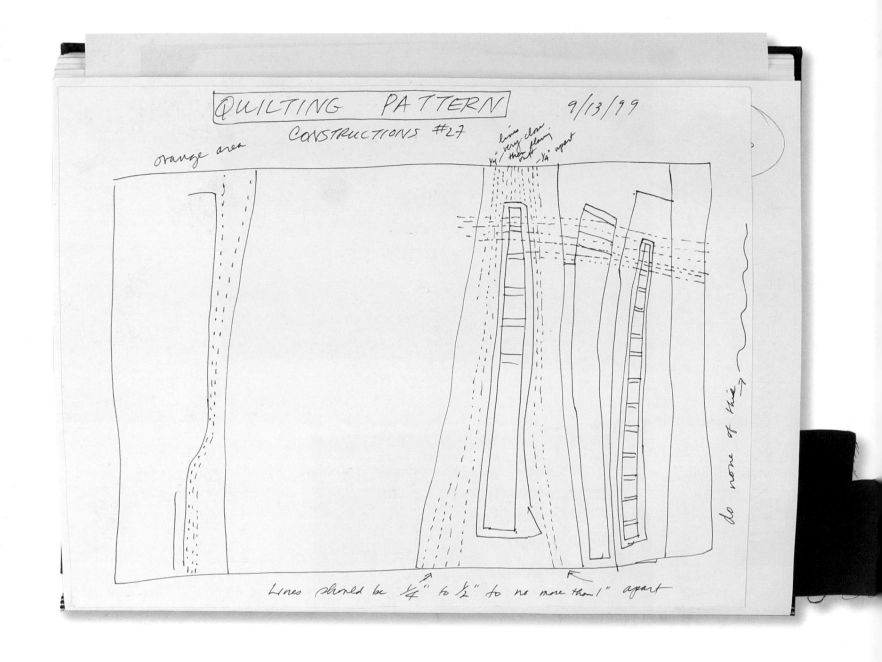

QUILTING   PATTERN          9/13/99
CONSTRUCTIONS #27

orange area

Lines should be ¼" to ½" to no more than 1" apart

## SEPTEMBER 16, 1999 | SKETCHBOOK NOTES

Constructions #27. *Began working once again on this quilt, September 9, 1999, after having returned August 18, 1999, from Australia, and after having spent weeks on accumulated correspondence.* CONTINUES ON SEPTEMBER 19 *I actually made parts of this quilt in 1998 while teaching and maybe a few parts in October 1997 while teaching at Quilting-by-the-Sound (QBS), Port Townsend, Washington. Anyway, I have basically made most of the "parts" for both this quilt, Constructions #27, and Constructions #20 in my spare time at workshops where I was teaching. [Note: Constructions #20 ultimately became Constructions #38, so there is no Constructions #20.] I always try to keep* BUSY *and not* WASTE TIME WHEN I AM TEACHING. *But the truth is I made lots of these "fabrics" and started Constructions #20 first but I had not finished it yet—ha! Yet—and it has been pinned to one of my primary work walls for over one-and-a-half years??? Not sure. But now—I will indeed finish it because in truth I love it. So I just have to do it—my favorite refrain.*

*Constructions #27*, ©1999.
73½″ × 54½″. 100 percent
cotton fabrics hand-dyed
by Nancy Crow. Fabrics
cut and machine-pieced
improvisationally by
Nancy Crow. Hand-quilted
by Marla Hattabaugh
with pattern denoted by
Nancy Crow.

*Constructions #29*, ©1999.
49" × 65". 100 percent
cotton fabrics hand-dyed
by Nancy Crow. Fabrics
cut and machine-pieced
improvisationally by
Nancy Crow. Hand-quilted
by Marla Hattabaugh
with pattern denoted by
Nancy Crow.

Constructions #30. *Again—what a* CHALLENGE! *Just creating abstract shapes and trying to like them. I am amazed at how hard, so hard I have struggled. Crying in despair. Other times—I can make abstract shapes work just like that—a snap! They come together as though meant to love one another. But this time—all is fighting—on the wall and inside me. Always inside me the fight that I am* NO GOOD; *that I am hard to like, to love. And then I long for my mother who loved me so much and who understood me. It is afternoon and I am determined to make this piece work somehow. I look out the window and I long to run outside but only so I can walk easily, without pain. My right knee* ACHES. *Each quilt is being made with such pain being endured in my right knee. I can stand only so long and then have to sit down.*

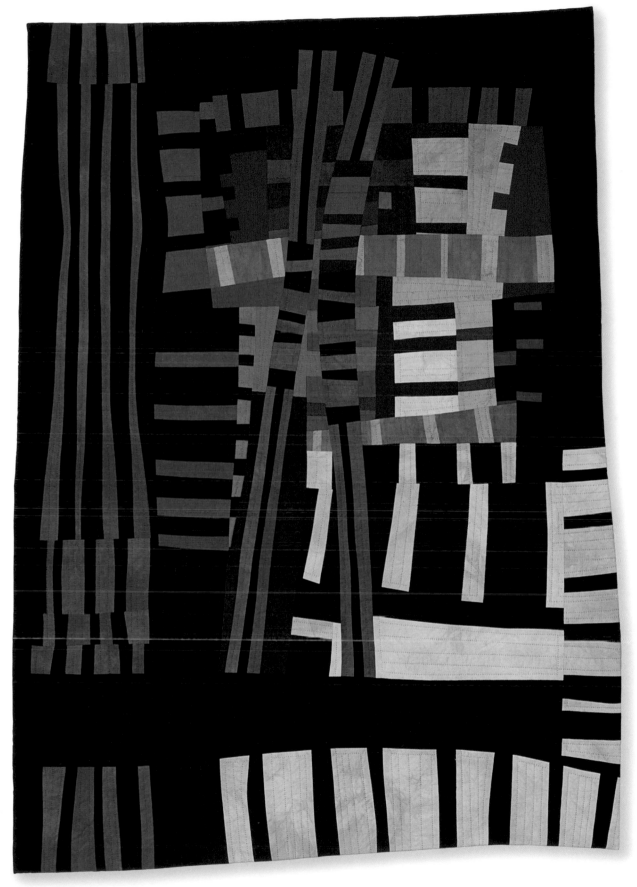

*Constructions #30,*
©1999–2000. 40" × 56".
100 percent cotton fabrics
hand-dyed by Nancy Crow.
Fabrics cut and machine-
pieced improvisationally by
Nancy Crow. Hand-quilted
by Marla Hattabaugh
with pattern denoted by
Nancy Crow.

***Constructions #31,***
©1999–2000. 18¼" × 40¾".
100 percent cotton fabrics
hand-dyed by Nancy Crow.
Fabrics cut and machine-
pieced improvisationally
by Nancy Crow. Hand-
quilted by Mildred Minchey
with pattern denoted by
Nancy Crow.

*Birch trees in Canada influenced the*
Constructions *series*

**Constructions #32**, ©2000.
46″ × 81″. 100 percent
cotton fabrics hand-dyed
by Nancy Crow. Fabrics
cut and machine-pieced
improvisationally by
Nancy Crow. Hand-quilted
by Marla Hattabaugh
with pattern denoted by
Nancy Crow.

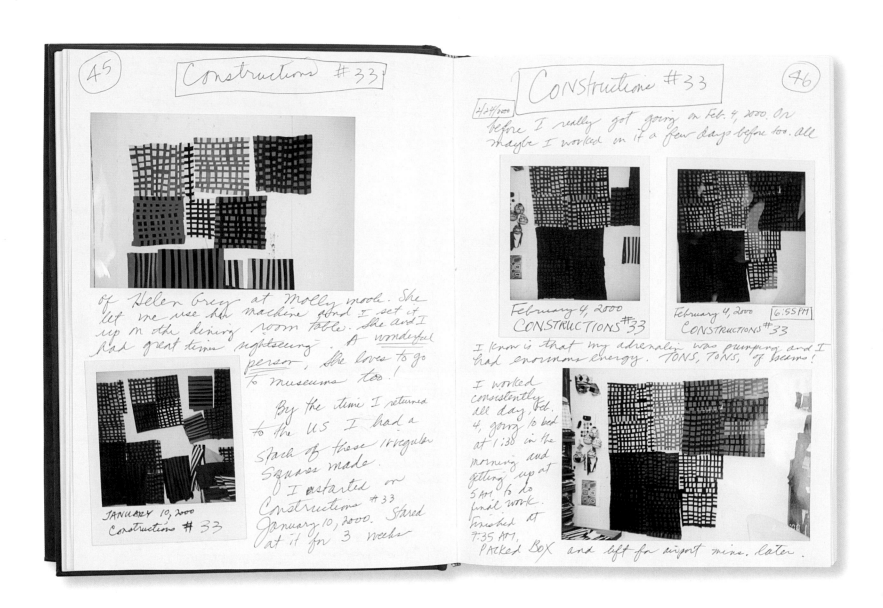

## 45

Constructions #33

of Helen Grey at Molly moole. She let me use her machine and I set it up in the dining room table. She and I had great time sightseeing. A wonderful person, she loves to go to museums too!

By the time I returned to the US I had a stack of these irregular squares made. I started on Constructions #33 January 10, 2000. Stared at it for 3 weeks

JANUARY 10, 2000 Construction #33

CONSTRUCTIONS #33

7/24/2000

before I really got going on Feb. 4, 2000. Or maybe I worked in it a few days before too. All

February 4, 2000 CONSTRUCTIONS #33

February 4, 2000 6:55 PM CONSTRUCTIONS #33

I know is that my adrenalin was pumping and I had enormous energy. TONS, TONS, of seams!

I worked consistently all day, Feb. 4, going to bed at 1:30 in the morning and getting up at 5 AM to do final work. Finished at 7:35 AM, PACKED BOX and left for airport mins. later.

*These sketchbook pages relate to Constructions #33.*

*Constructions #33*,
©1999–2000. 65¼″ × 60″.
100 percent cotton fabrics
hand-dyed by Nancy Crow.
Fabrics cut and machine-
pieced improvisationally by
Nancy Crow. Hand-quilted
by Marla Hattabaugh
with pattern denoted by
Nancy Crow.

*Constructions #34*, ©2000. 17″ × 18½″. 100 percent cotton fabrics hand-dyed by Nancy Crow. Fabrics cut and machine-pieced improvisationally by Nancy Crow. Hand-quilted by Marla Hattabaugh with pattern denoted by Nancy Crow.

*Constructions #35*, ©2000. 7″ × 9¾″. 100 percent cotton fabrics hand-dyed by Nancy Crow. Fabrics cut and machine-pieced improvisationally by Nancy Crow. Hand-quilted by Marla Hattabaugh with pattern denoted by Nancy Crow.

*Constructions #36*, ©2000. 7″ × 13″. 100 percent cotton fabrics hand-dyed by Nancy Crow. Fabrics cut and machine-pieced improvisationally by Nancy Crow. Hand-quilted by Marla Hattabaugh with pattern denoted by Nancy Crow.

RIGHT *A half-timber house in Denmark. I relate these images to* Constructions #26, Constructions #33 *through* Constructions #36, Constructions #39, Constructions #43, *and* Constructions #45 *(see pages 203, 213–214, 225, 231, and 233).*

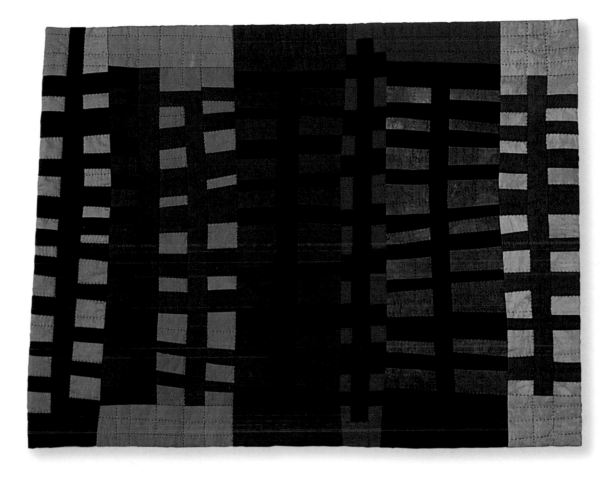

*Constructions #37*, ©2000. 24″ × 19″. 100 percent cotton fabrics hand-dyed by Nancy Crow. Fabrics cut and machine-pieced improvisationally by Nancy Crow. Hand-quilted by Marla Hattabaugh with pattern denoted by Nancy Crow.

FROM TOP LEFT, PHOTO 1 *The Poling barn as it looked when given to us by the Landis family, who had bought the Poling farm which is adjacent to ours. The barn was an outright gift and allowed us to spend our money on its renovation.* PHOTO 2 *Back on our farm, we first had to create a road extending from our lane and leading out into the field where the barn would be newly situated.* PHOTO 3 *I-beams were placed under and inside the barn to stabilize it for moving. This photograph contains those squares/rectangles I love!* PHOTO 4 *Inside the barn, looking down onto the placement of the I-beams. Taking out the old flooring, removing the boulders on which the posts of the barn rested, and inserting the new I-beams took more time (two weeks) than the actual moving of the barn to its new site.*

# RENOVATING THE POLING BARN INTO THE CROW TIMBER FRAME BARN

5

6

7

8

I HAVE BEEN WORKING on the *Constructions* series since 1996. The major influence for the series has been my study and evaluation of the exquisitely proportioned relationships between the interior beams and the flat vertical and horizontal boards of the huge 1880s timber-frame barn that now stands on our farm.

In making the quilts in this series, I have combined my love of the proportions found in this barn with my love of color, shape, line, and graphic intensity. I have always worked out of personal experience and from observations made in my environment. The barn renovation has had an enormous impact on my thinking and emotions.

The renovation of a 1880s barn into the Crow Timber Frame Barn was the culmination of five factors. First, I wanted to have a first-rate teaching facility that included a well-equipped surface-design classroom. Second, I wanted to have another large studio, with enough wall space to accommodate large ideas. Third was the fact that we had saved enough money over a ten-year period to fund a large-scale project of this kind. Fourth was the timely and miraculous gift of a huge timber-frame barn that was located nearby and that was in excellent condition, making it feasible to move and renovate. And last, the threesome—my husband and two sons—had the knowledge, skills, desire, and enthusiasm to undertake this four-year-long project and see it through to completion.

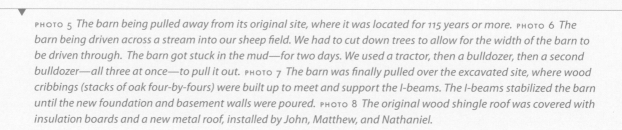

PHOTO 5 *The barn being pulled away from its original site, where it was located for 115 years or more.* PHOTO 6 *The barn being driven across a stream into our sheep field. We had to cut down trees to allow for the width of the barn to be driven through. The barn got stuck in the mud—for two days. We used a tractor, then a bulldozer, then a second bulldozer—all three at once—to pull it out.* PHOTO 7 *The barn was finally pulled over the excavated site, where wood cribbings (stacks of oak four-by-fours) were built up to meet and support the I-beams. The I-beams stabilized the barn until the new foundation and basement walls were poured.* PHOTO 8 *The original wood shingle roof was covered with insulation boards and a new metal roof, installed by John, Matthew, and Nathaniel.*

9

10

14

11

12

13

15

FROM TOP LEFT, PHOTO 9 *The first layer of the new wood floor on the upper level being laid down on the diagonal. It was made entirely of tulip poplar. The second layer to go over the top was laid straight, east to west, and was made of quarter-sawn sycamore we ordered form Ohio's Amish territory.* PHOTO 10 *New, solid oak joists in place, supporting the basement ceiling, which is also the new upper-level floor* PHOTO 11 *We preserved the entire barn by encasing it in new insulation, new siding, and a new roof. From inside, only the original wood boards are visible. They are a mix of American chestnut and beech—all old-growth timber. The new siding was hemlock, which was specially milled for the barn.* PHOTO 12 *The new floor and the original wood siding as seen inside the barn.*

16

17

18

PHOTO 13 *We used sandstone blocks like this one to hold the huge posts of the porch built out from the kitchen on the west side of the barn. They were hand-made in the 1880s and came from the original Yellow Barn on our property.* PHOTO 14 *The original wood shingle roof as seen inside the barn and left undisturbed.* PHOTO 15 *A 36-foot by 36-foot two-story addition on the south side of the barn being built to house a kitchen, a dining room, and bathrooms upstairs, with a surface-design room, complete with sinks, downstairs.* PHOTO 16 *The completed exterior.* PHOTO 17 *The surface-design room in the basement.* PHOTO 18 *My studio inside the timber frame barn.*

*Part of my basket collection in Studio #1. The patterns on these baskets inspired aspects of the Constructions series.*

*Constructions #38*, ©2000.
77″ × 38″. 100 percent
cotton fabrics hand-dyed
by Nancy Crow. Fabrics
cut and machine-pieced
improvisationally by
Nancy Crow. Hand-quilted
by Marla Hattabaugh
with pattern denoted by
Nancy Crow.

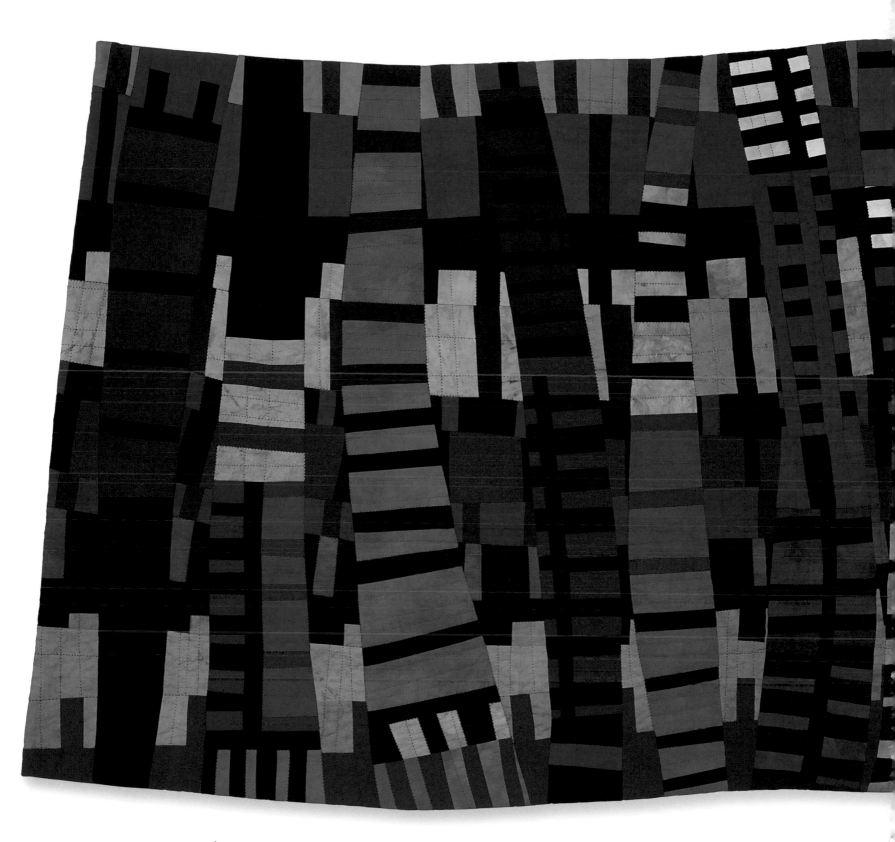

*Finally had a breakthrough since I have been working on this quilt for two years. What a struggle. I first called it* Constructions #20 *but frankly it fits in now as* Constructions #38 *(in the sequence of my numbering the* Constructions *series) because this was how I want to resolve it—wild! Gutsy! Red, blue, brown, orange, green, black.* CONTINUES ON APRIL 21 *Started working again on April 18 and it has been a monumental struggle. First nothing seemed to be coming together in this piece in which the colors are nearly* GARISH—*the oranges taking up huge spaces. But this is where my heart and mind are leading me so I am following. If I relax and stop after a few hours, I can come back with a fresh eye and results flow at least for a short time. I suppose I need lots more practice working on something this disjointed. I am playing the same song on my stereo over and over . . . over and over . . . because it seems to calm me.* REPETITION CALMS ME. *I have been exceedingly emotional these days—crying easily like I did in years* BEFORE *my mother died. After she died, it seemed I couldn't cry anymore. I decided to be more stoic. But lately, I cry easily. I feel so tender toward both my sons who I absolutely* ADORE. *They are such fine human beings, just like my mother was.*

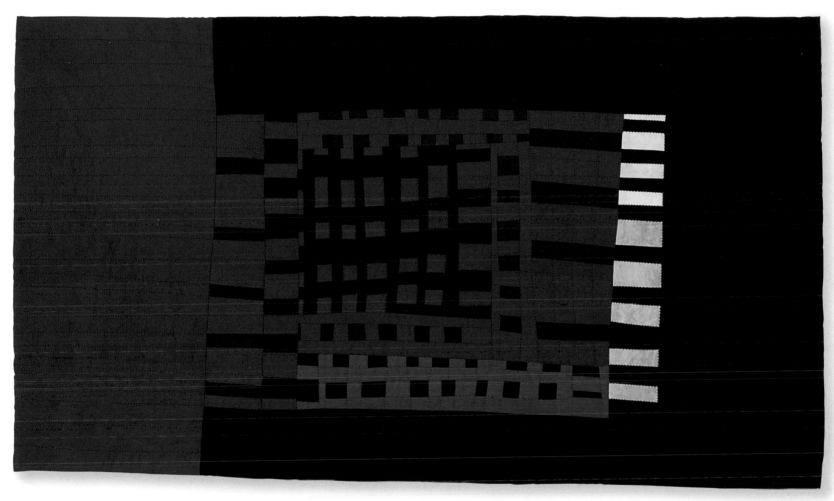

*Constructions #39,* ©2000.
43″ × 25″. 100 percent
cotton fabrics hand-dyed
by Nancy Crow. Fabrics
cut and machine-pieced
improvisationally by
Nancy Crow. Hand-quilted
by Marla Hattabaugh
with pattern denoted by
Nancy Crow.

*Constructions #40*, ©2000.
33″ × 88½″. 100 percent
cotton fabrics hand-dyed
by Nancy Crow. Fabrics
cut and machine-pieced
improvisationally by
Nancy Crow. Hand-quilted
by Marla Hattabaugh
with pattern denoted by
Nancy Crow.

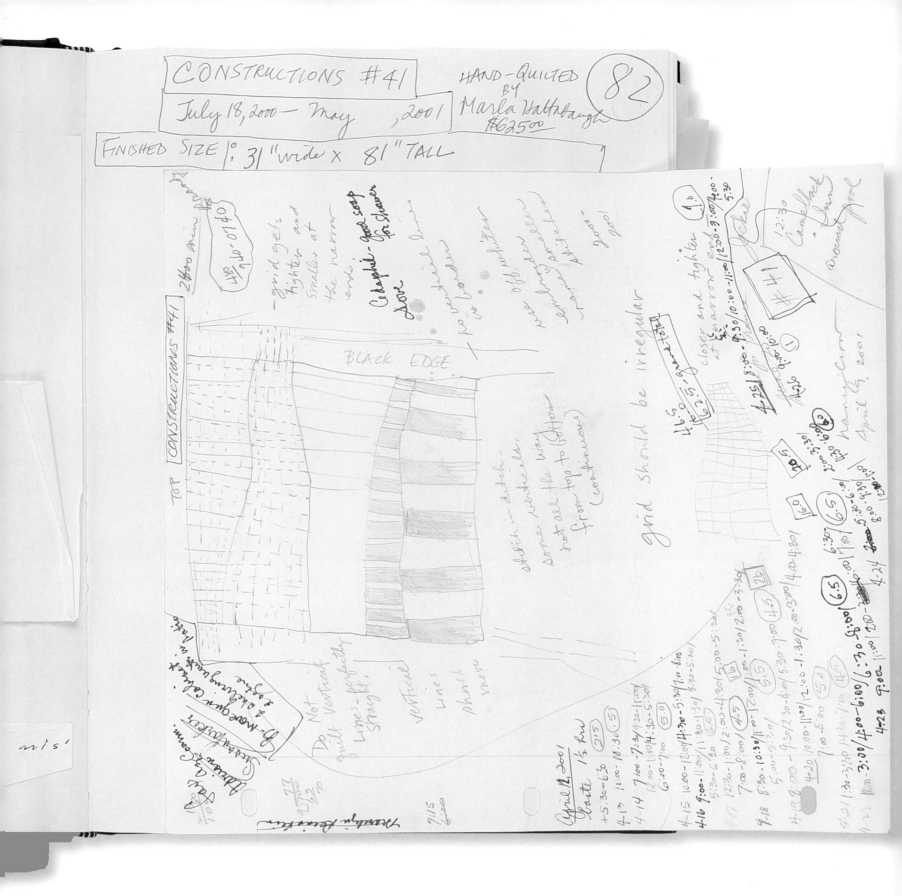

Instructions for the hand-quilting patterns that were sent to Marla
Hattabaugh for Constructions #41. Notice that she kept her hours
noted on the side of the page, along with other random notes.

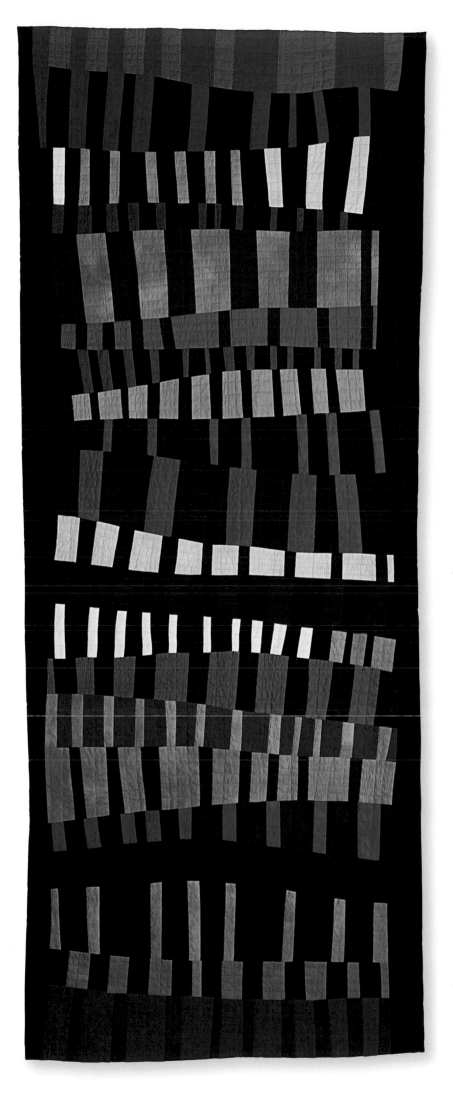

***Constructions #41,***
©2000–2001. 31″ × 81″.
100 percent cotton fabrics
hand-dyed by Nancy Crow.
Fabrics cut and machine-
pieced improvisationally by
Nancy Crow. Hand-quilted
by Marla Hattabaugh
with pattern denoted by
Nancy Crow.

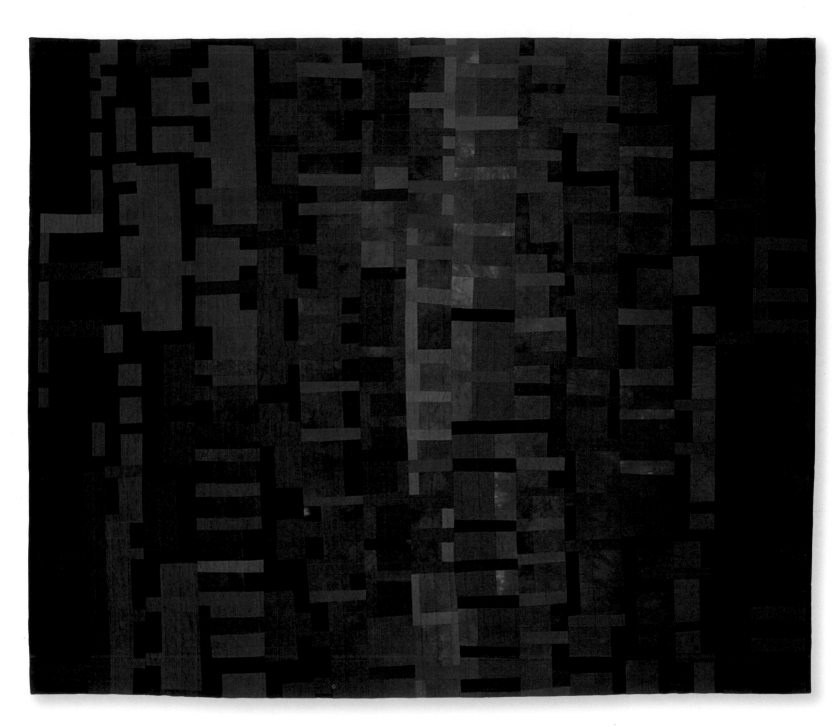

**Constructions #42,**
©2000–2001. 76½″ × 64½″.
100 percent cotton fabrics
hand-dyed by Nancy Crow.
Fabrics cut and machine-
pieced improvisationally by
Nancy Crow. Hand-quilted
by Marla Hattabaugh
with pattern denoted by
Nancy Crow.

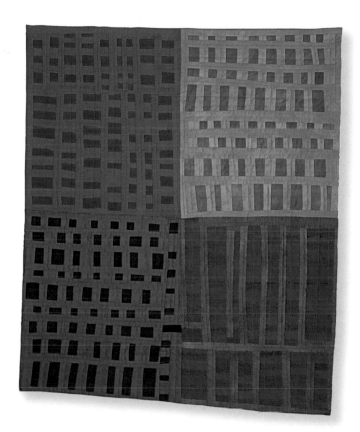

**Constructions #43**, ©2001. 32″ × 38¼″. 100 percent cotton fabrics hand-dyed by Nancy Crow. Fabrics cut and machine-pieced improvisationally by Nancy Crow. Hand-quilted by Marla Hattabaugh with pattern denoted by Nancy Crow.

*Rosalie Gascoigne, one of my favorite artists—one who I respect so highly— states, "You're bored to extinction if you repeat yourself."*

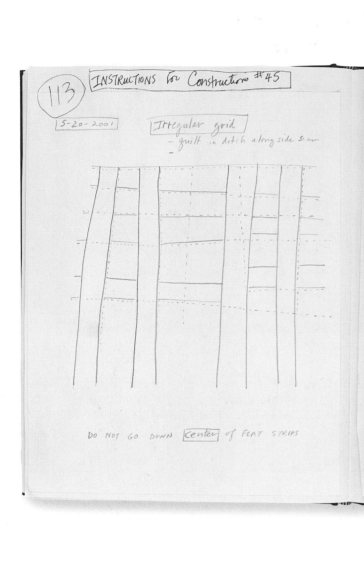

INSTRUCTIONS For Constructions #45

5-20-2001

Irregular grid
– quilt in ditch along side seam

DO NOT GO DOWN Center of FLAT STRIPS

RIGHT *Detail,* Constructions #45. ABOVE *Instructions for hand-quilting* Constructions #45, *emphasizing stitching "in-the-ditch".*

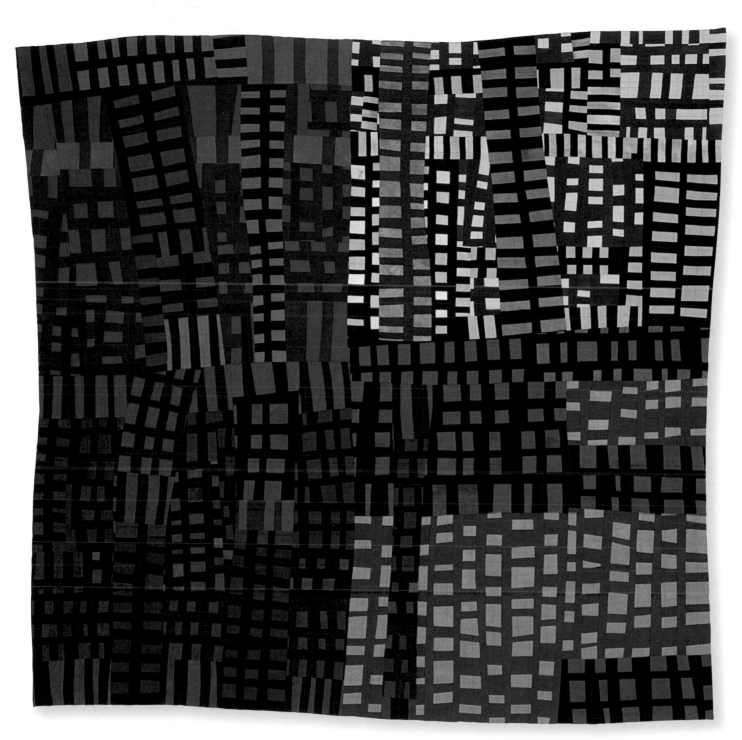

*Constructions #45*, ©2001.
63" × 64". 100 percent
cotton fabrics hand-dyed
by Nancy Crow. Fabrics
cut and machine-pieced
improvisationally by
Nancy Crow. Hand-quilted
by Marla Hattabaugh
with pattern denoted by
Nancy Crow.

*Constructions #46* ©2001. 15½″ × 17⅝″. 100 percent cotton fabrics hand-dyed by Nancy Crow. Fabrics cut and machine-pieced improvisationally by Nancy Crow. Hand-quilted by Marla Hattabaugh with pattern denoted by Nancy Crow.

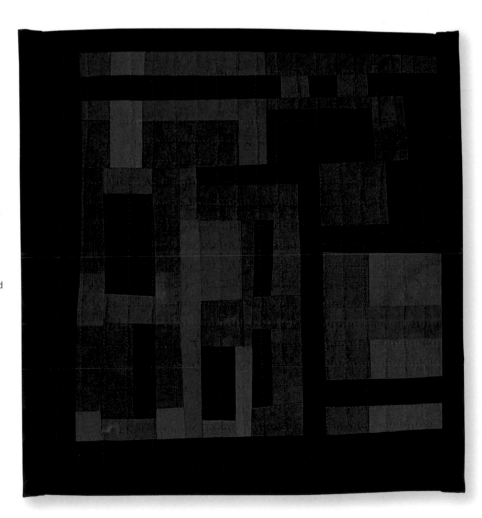

*Constructions #47*, ©2001. 17½″ × 18¼″. 100 percent cotton fabrics hand-dyed by Nancy Crow. Fabrics cut and machine-pieced improvisationally by Nancy Crow. Hand-quilted by Marla Hattabaugh with pattern denoted by Nancy Crow.

***Constructions #48***, ©2001.
19⅜″ × 22″. 100 percent
cotton fabrics hand-dyed
by Nancy Crow. Fabrics
cut and machine-pieced
improvisationally by
Nancy Crow. Hand-quilted
by Marla Hattabaugh
with pattern denoted by
Nancy Crow.

SEPTEMBER 4, 2001 | SKETCHBOOK NOTES

*I am working in my studio this morning, finding my footing. Always so, so hard to discover or
find. Hours of discouragement. Days of discouragement. Avoiding opening door into my studio.
Afraid I can't find my footing. But it is coming! I can sense it is starting to happen. And as a
result my energy level is surging.* CONTINUES ON SEPTEMBER 5 *Worked hard yesterday. Finished*
Constructions #48 *and* Constructions #46 *and* Constructions #47 *on Tuesday.*

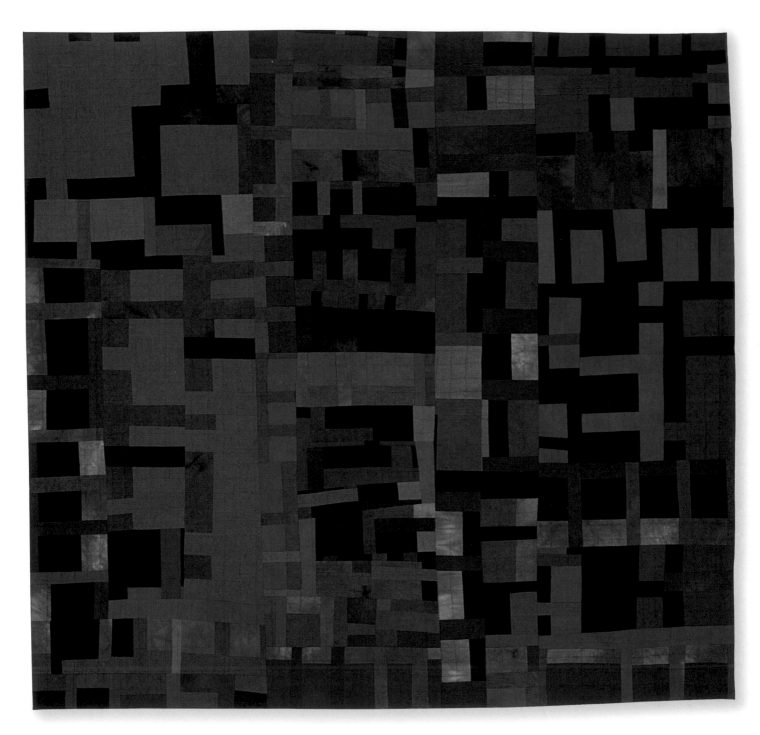

*Constructions #49*,
©2001–2002. 58" × 55¾".
100 percent cotton fabrics
hand-dyed by Nancy Crow.
Fabrics cut and machine-
pieced improvisationally by
Nancy Crow. Hand-quilted
by Marla Hattabaugh
with pattern denoted by
Nancy Crow.

**Constructions #50**,
©2001–2002. 46″ × 40½″.
100 percent cotton fabrics
hand-dyed by Nancy Crow.
Fabrics cut and machine-
pieced improvisationally by
Nancy Crow. Hand-quilted
by Marla Hattabaugh
with pattern denoted by
Nancy Crow.

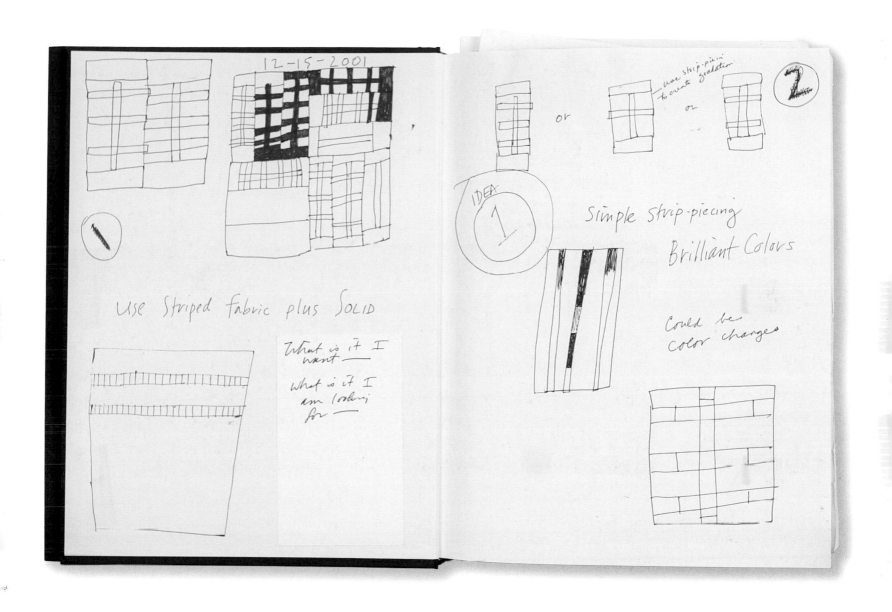

CONTINUES ON JANUARY 11

JANUARY 1, 2002 | SKETCHBOOK NOTES

*My ideas flood me and I guess I should just draw them down instead of trying to get just one idea down and then execute it in fabric. I am trying to be methodical but in actuality—this is not working at all. I am piling up ideas on bits of paper or on 4" by 6" blank cards and then as the piles grow and get shuffled, I totally lose track of what I was doing.* CONTINUES ON JANUARY 11 *What is it I want? What is it I am looking for?* I AM TRYING, TRYING, TRYING TO FOCUS. MY BRAIN WHIRLS AND WHIRLS WITH IDEAS. SO MANY IDEAS—AND I HAVE TO SOMEHOW GET THEM CHANNELED INTO A FOCUS. *I almost did not finish making this piece as the more I worked on it, the more I* HATED *it. It took on its own energy and tried to "outfox" me. I had intended to make a large 80" by 80" top, but somehow it ended up tall, very tall, and narrow. John had to help pin it to the wall going up and down the step ladder . . .* NOW I LOVE THIS QUILT!

*Constructions #54*, ©2002.
39" × 99". 100 percent
cotton fabrics hand-cyed
by Nancy Crow. Fabrics
cut and machine-pieced
improvisationally by
Nancy Crow. Hand-quilted
by Marla Hattabaugh
with pattern denotec by
Nancy Crow.

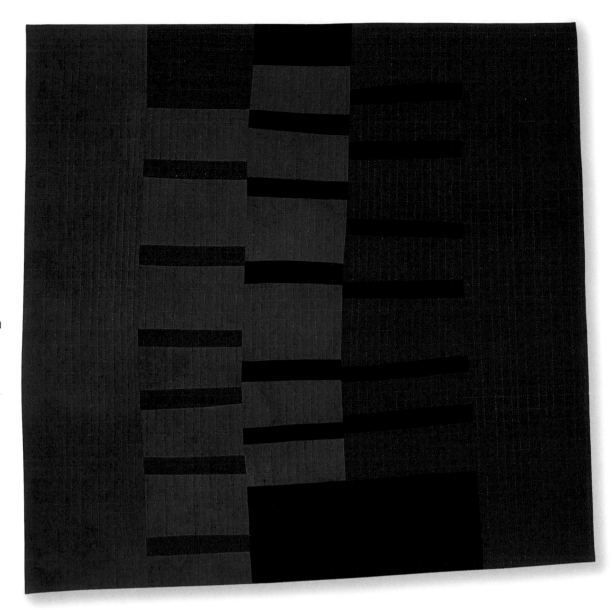

**Constructions #55,** ©2002.
37" × 37". 100 percent
cotton fabrics hand-dyed
by Nancy Crow. Fabrics
cut and machine-pieced
improvisationally by
Nancy Crow. Hand-quilted
by Marla Hattabaugh
with pattern denoted by
Nancy Crow.

ABOVE *This quilt was based on my small study,* Constructions #25, *made in April 1999. It actually preceded* Constructions #54, *but I had to rip it apart as I did not like the proportions.* RIGHT *Instructions for hand-quilting a very fine grid for* Constructions #55, Constructions #56, *and* Constructions #57.

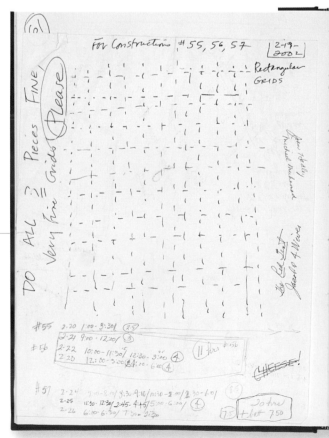

*Constructions #56*, ©2002. 13¾" × 19". 100 percent cotton fabrics hand-dyed by Nancy Crow. Fabrics cut and machine-pieced improvisationally by Nancy Crow. Hand-quilted by Marla Hattabaugh with pattern denoted by Nancy Crow.

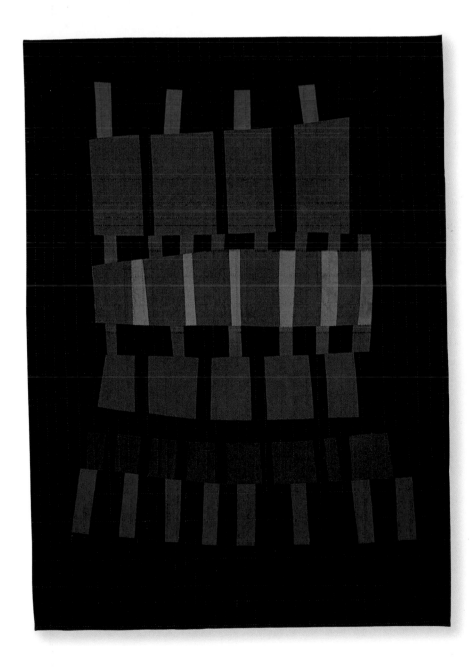

*Constructions #57*, ©2002. 26½" × 38". 100 percent cotton fabrics hand-dyed by Nancy Crow. Fabrics cut and machine-pieced improvisationally by Nancy Crow. Hand-quilted by Marla Hattabaugh with pattern denoted by Nancy Crow.

TOP Constructions #58 *under construction in Studio #1.*
ABOVE LEFT *Woven side of a home in South Africa. This image*
*influenced* Constructions #58. RIGHT *Sketchbook drawings*
*denoting quilting pattern for* Constructions #58.

***Constructions #58***, ©2002. 76″ × 87″. 100 percent cotton fabrics hand-dyed by Nancy Crow. Fabrics cut and machine-pieced improvisationally by Nancy Crow. Hand-quilted by Marla Hattabaugh with pattern denoted by Nancy Crow.

FEBRUARY 28, 2002 | SKETCHBOOK NOTES

*Constructions #58. Picking up where I left off from parts made during workshop at Quilting by the Lake (1998?). All the finished parts have been sitting in my studio since then.* CONTINUES ON MARCH 5 *What I mean is that I made parts with only* BLACK *and three other colors—red, reddish brown, and off-white. I am now adding twelve other colors and when all parts are made, I will arrange the bands on the wall till I like the arrangement. The best arrangement always depends on colors combined with values. Value always is difficult, or I should say more tricky, to reconcile in creating compositions.* CONTINUES ON JULY 11 *This is by far the heaviest quilt (due to all the seams) I have every made! My back just* ACHES *and* ACHES. *Went to bed at midnight, too tired to think but exhilarated. Just wrote out notes for the quilting pattern. I do hope Marla can do what I want. It will be difficult because of all the seams.* CONTINUES ON AUGUST 15 *Just took this quilt out of box. It is (looks) magnificent!*

*Strip-pieced fabrics being prepared for* Constructions #59 *and* Constructions #60. *Pinned to the wall are small wool bags from Chiapas, Mexico. The strip-piecing was influenced by the multi-colored ribbons on the hat from Chamula, Mexico. In the photo above, the hat sits on the corner of the table at the right.* Constructions #59 *became the study for* Constructions #60.

***Constructions #59***, ©2002.
35½″ × 36½″. 100 percent
cotton fabrics hand-dyed
by Nancy Crow. Fabrics
cut and machine-pieced
improvisationally by
Nancy Crow. Hand-quilted
by Marla Hattabaugh
with pattern denoted by
Nancy Crow.

*Constructions #60*, ©2002.
73" × 72". 100 percent
cotton fabrics hand-dyed
by Nancy Crow. Fabrics
cut and machine-pieced
improvisationally by
Nancy Crow. Hand-quilted
by Marla Hattabaugh
with pattern denoted by
Nancy Crow.

*Constructions #61*, ©2003.
39" × 39". 100 percent
cotton fabrics hand-dyed
by Nancy Crow. Fabrics
cut and machine-pieced
improvisationally by
Nancy Crow. Hand-quilted
by Marla Hattabaugh
with pattern denoted by
Nancy Crow.

LEFT *On the table are piles of finished strip-piecing waiting to be used.
On the wall are Guatemalan belts and a* huipile *below an embroidery
from the Mapola Project in South Africa.*

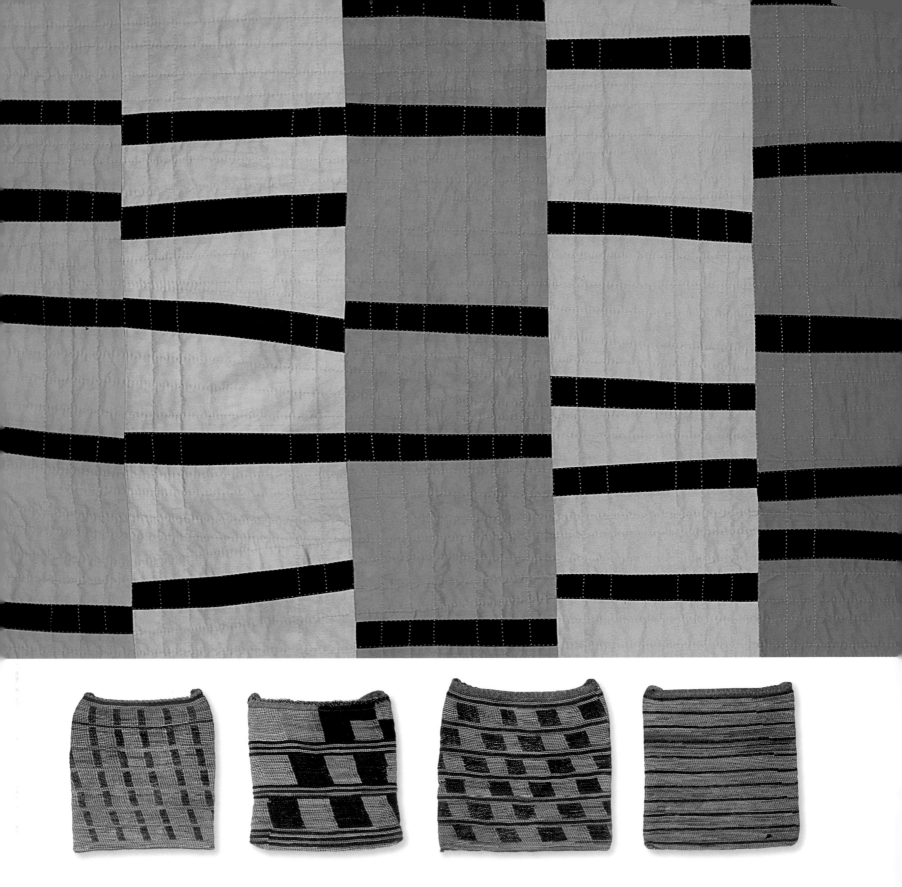

JULY 11, 2002 | SKETCHBOOK NOTES

*Constructions #62. I started on July 13, 2002. Somehow I thought I would work on a different quilt altogether but I had just dyed egg yolk yellows and I wanted to work with those incredible yellows. I'd had such bad luck with my dyeing during the cold months of 2002 (January, February, March) and was beginning to think I did not know how to dye my RICH colors. But as the weather warmed up I discovered two things—room temperature in my dye room needed to be 70°F minimum—it was too cold for dyes to set. AND I also was not using enough dye per yard nor enough soda ash to fix the dyes. Ann Johnston helped me with all this when I showed her my ugly results—washed out, grayish colors.* ABOVE *Very, very fine banana-fiber bags, purchased at the Auckland Museum, New Zealand, in 2003. I relate these to Constructions #62. Collection of Nancy Crow.*

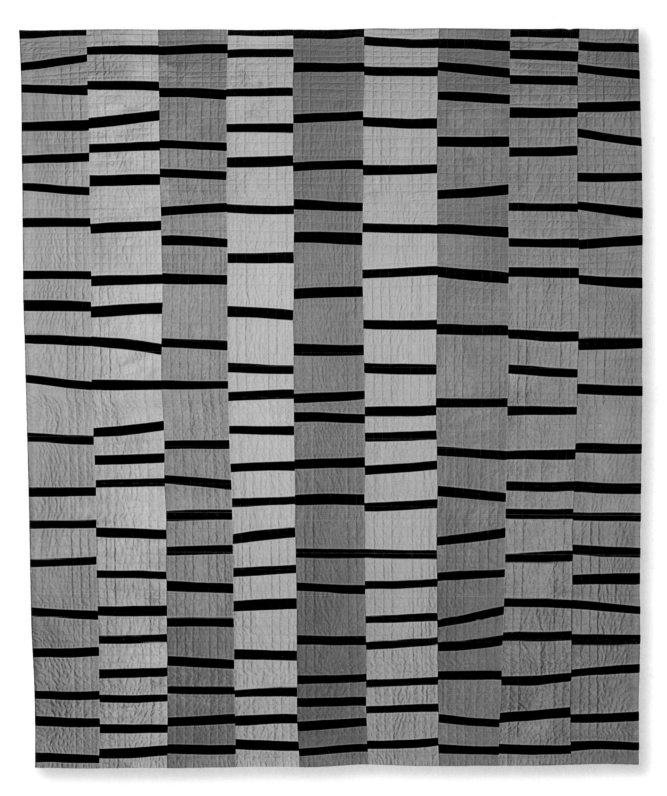

***Constructions #62***, ©2002.
71½″ × 87″. 100 percent
cotton fabrics hand-dyed
by Nancy Crow. Fabrics
cut and machine-pieced
improvisationally by
Nancy Crow. Hand-quilted
by Marla Hattabaugh
with pattern denoted by
Nancy Crow.

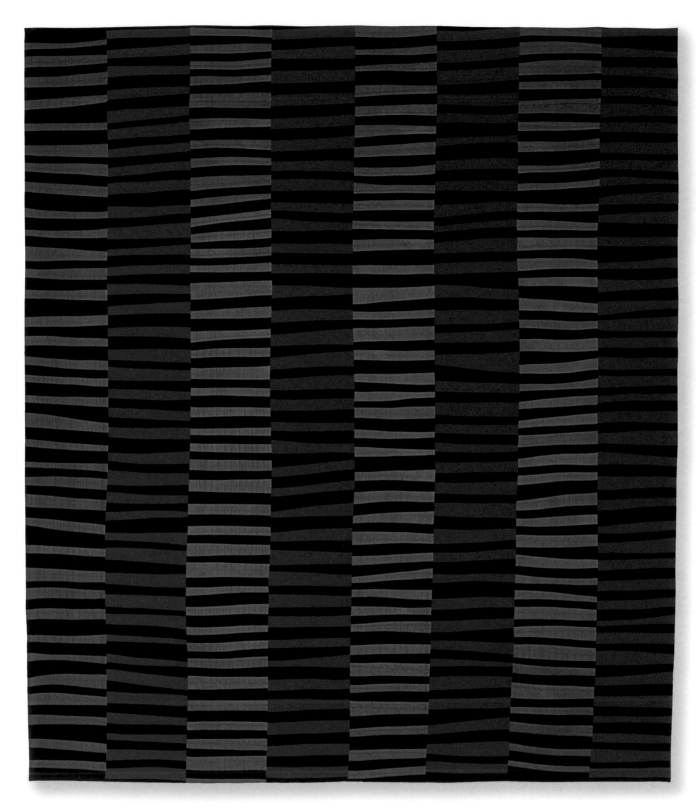

***Constructions #63,***
©2003–2004. 77″ × 89¼″.
100 percent cotton fabrics
hand-dyed by Nancy Crow.
Fabrics cut and machine-
pieced improvisationally by
Nancy Crow. Hand-quilted
by Marla Hattabaugh
with pattern denoted by
Nancy Crow.

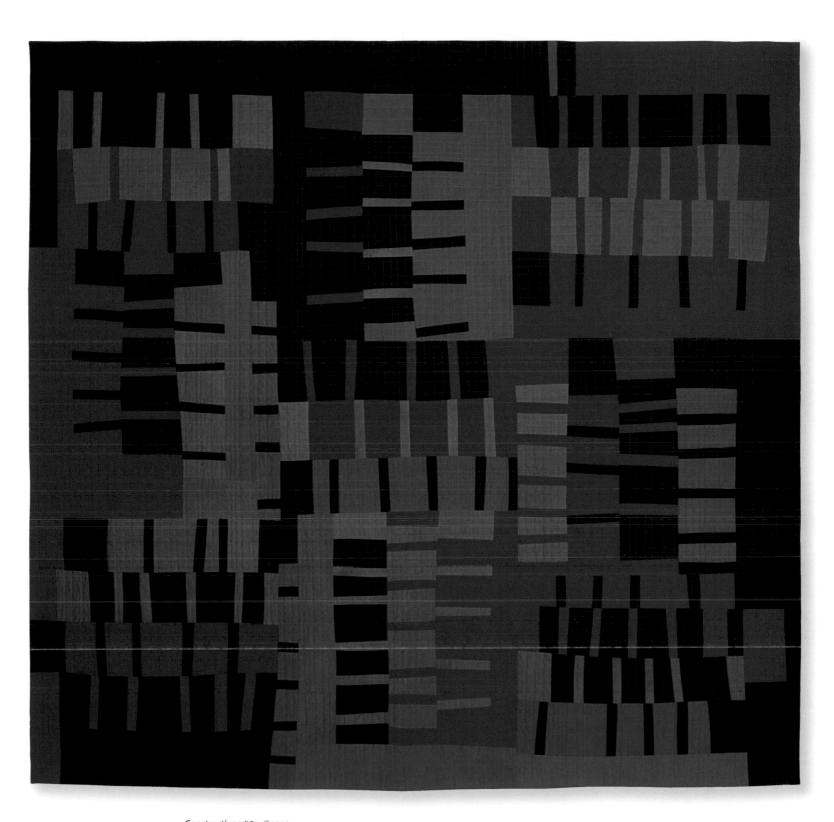

***Constructions #64***, ©2002.
89″ × 87½″. 100 percent
cotton fabrics hand-dyed
by Nancy Crow. Fabrics
cut and machine-pieced
improvisationally by
Nancy Crow. Hand-quilted
by Marla Hattabaugh
with pattern denoted by
Nancy Crow.

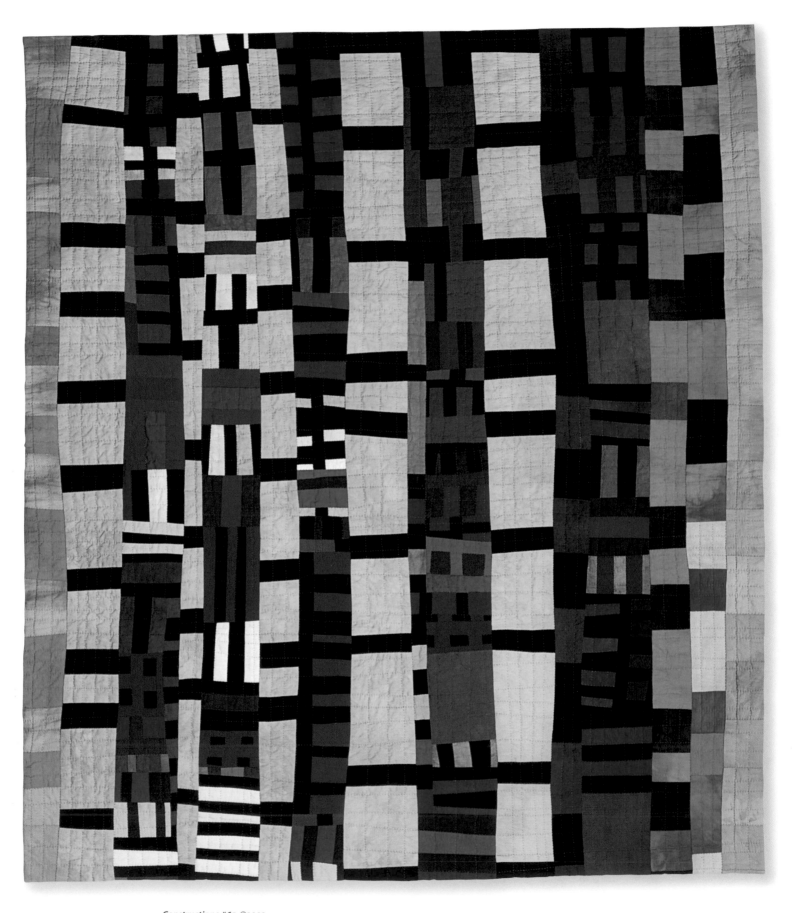

*Constructions #65*, ©2003.
42½" × 49". 100 percent
cotton fabrics hand-dyed
by Nancy Crow. Fabrics
cut and machine-pieced
improvisationally by
Nancy Crow. Hand-quilted
by Marla Hattabaugh
with pattern denoted by
Nancy Crow.

***Constructions #66***, ©2003.
41″ × 46″. 100 percent
cotton fabrics hand-dyed
by Nancy Crow. Fabrics
cut and machine-pieced
improvisationally by
Nancy Crow. Hand-quilted
by Marla Hattabaugh
with pattern denoted by
Nancy Crow.

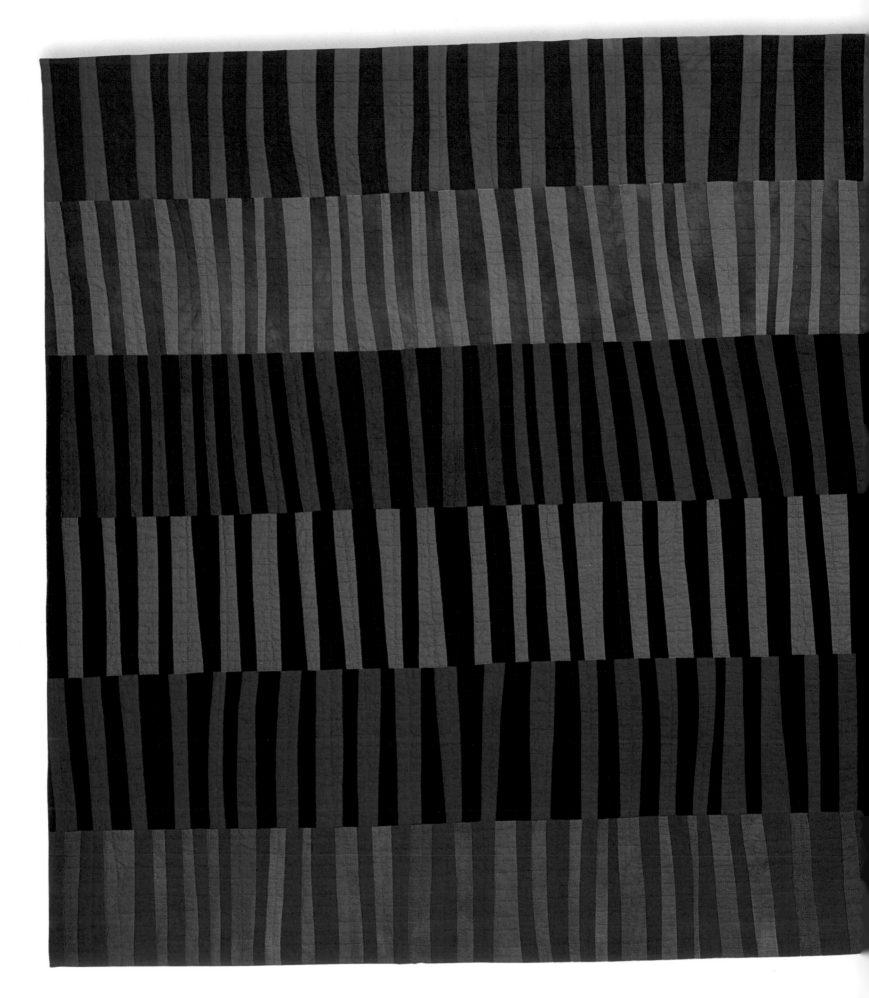

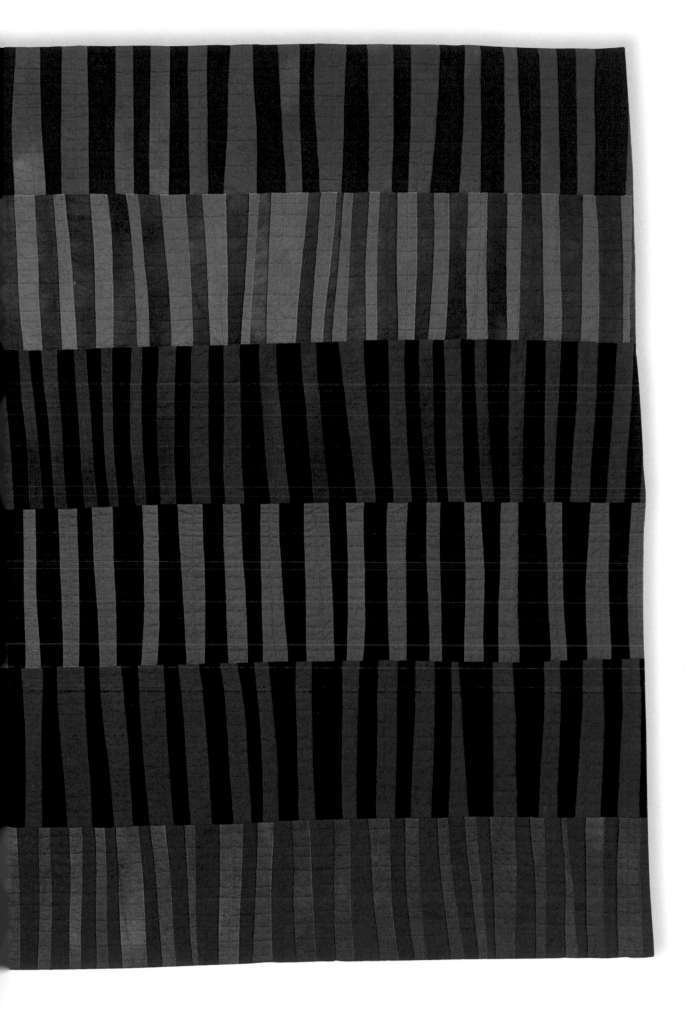

*Constructions #67*, ©2003.
54¼" × 87¼". 100 percent
cotton fabrics hand-dyed
by Nancy Crow. Fabrics
cut and machine-pieced
improvisationally by
Nancy Crow. Hand-quilted
by Marla Hattabaugh
with pattern denoted by
Nancy Crow

*Constructions #68*, ©2003. 20⅝″ × 30¼″. 100 percent cotton fabrics hand-dyed by Nancy Crow. Fabrics cut and machine-pieced improvisationally by Nancy Crow. Hand-quilted by Marla Hattabaugh with pattern denoted by Nancy Crow

*Constructions #69*, ©2003. 42″ × 25″. 100 percent cotton fabrics hand-dyed by Nancy Crow. Fabrics cut and machine-pieced improvisationally by Nancy Crow. Hand-quilted by Marla Hattabaugh with pattern denoted by Nancy Crow.

***Constructions #70***, ©2003.
36¼″ × 47½″. 100 percent
cotton fabrics hand-dyed
by Nancy Crow. Fabrics
cut and machine-pieced
improvisationally by
Nancy Crow. Hand-quilted
by Marla Hattabaugh
with pattern denoted by
Nancy Crow.

*Constructions #71*, ©2003.
37¾" × 65¾". 100 percent
cotton fabrics hand-dyed
by Nancy Crow. Fabrics
cut and machine-pieced
improvisationally by
Nancy Crow. Hand-quilted
by Marla Hattabaugh
with pattern denoted by
Nancy Crow.

*Constructions #72*, ©2003.
58″ × 96″. 100 percent
cotton fabrics hand-dyed
by Nancy Crow. Fabrics
cut and machine-pieced
improvisationally by
Nancy Crow. Hand-quilted
by Marla Hattabaugh
with pattern denoted by
Nancy Crow.

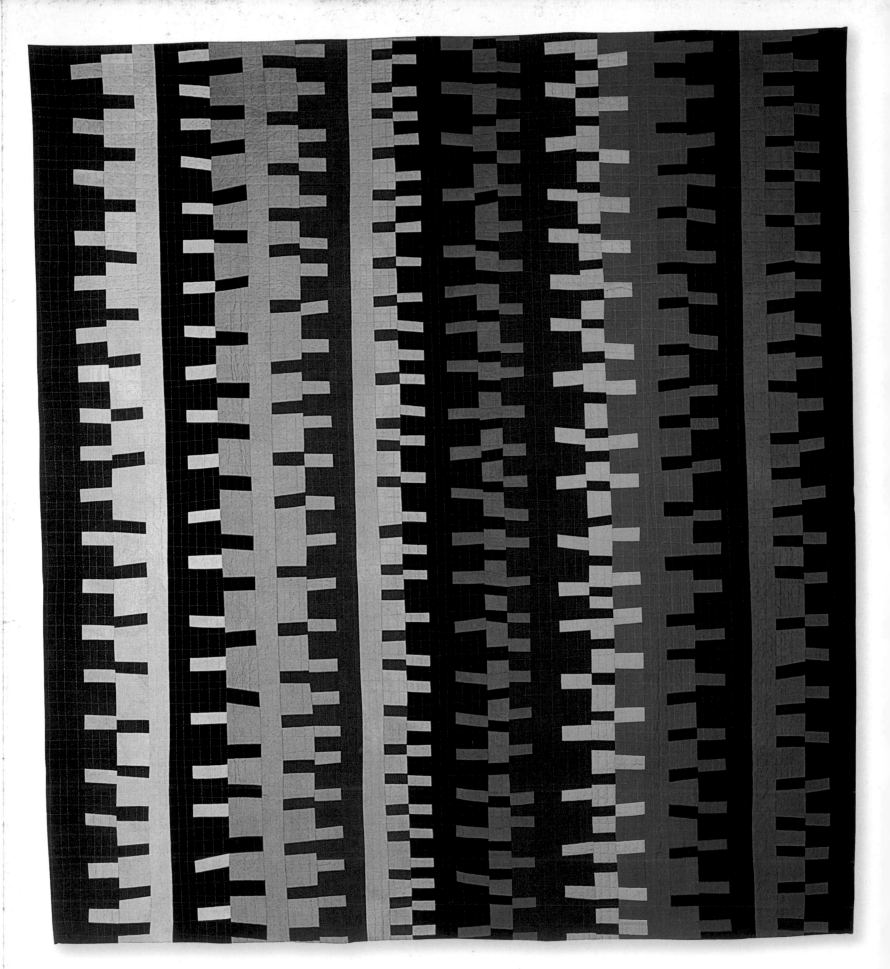

*Constructions #73*,
©2003–2004. 75½" × 84¾".
100 percent cotton fabrics
hand-dyed by Nancy Crow.
Fabrics cut and machine-
pieced improvisationally by
Nancy Crow. Hand-quilted
by Marla Hattabaugh
with pattern denoted by
Nancy Crow.

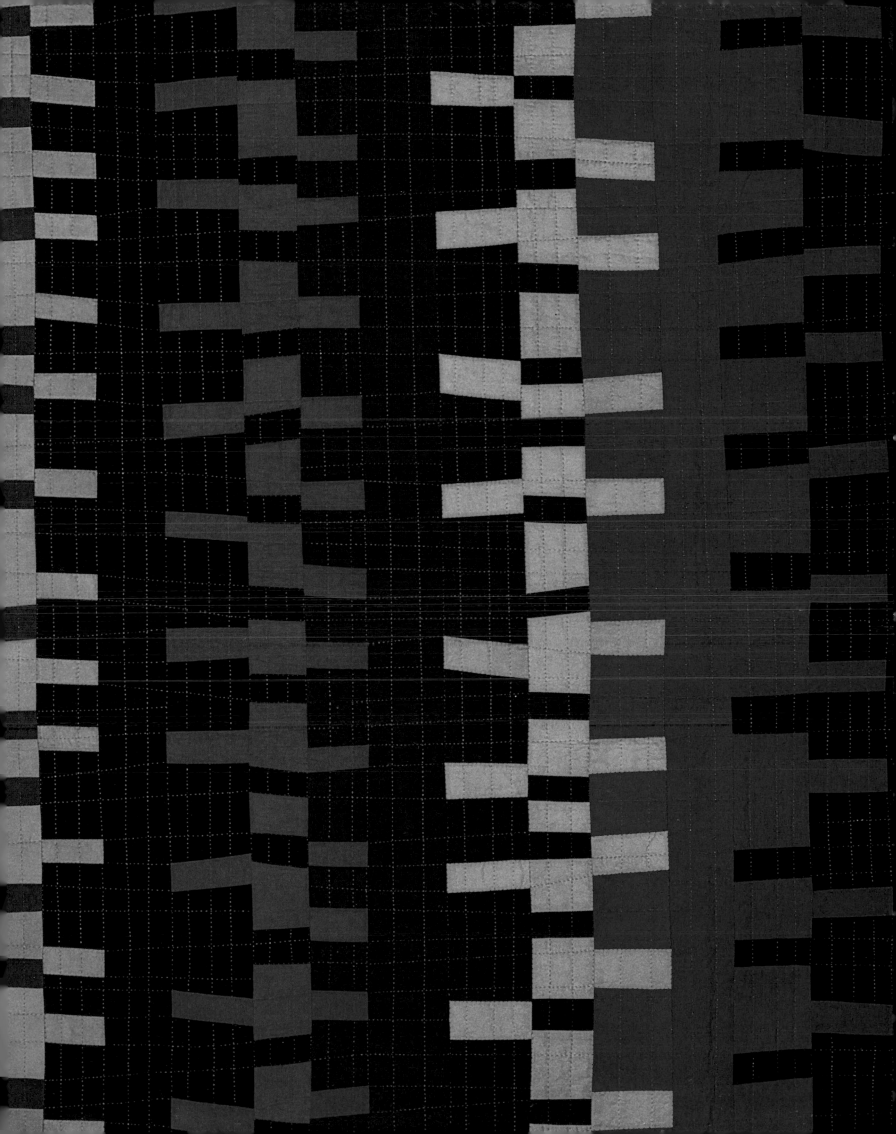

RIGHT Constructions #73 *started on one of my work walls in the Crow Timber Frame Barn. I spaced vertical strips to help get an idea of final size and color placement.* ABOVE *Pinned up on the wall at right is a textile from Solola, Guatemala. I particularly like the staccato rhythm of Solola textiles.* LEFT *Bark cloth from New Guinea with patterning that I love and can relate to* Constructions #73. *Collection of Nancy Crow.*

# VERTICALS AND HORIZONTALS

Always! I am always interested in PURE SHAPE and PURE LINE and their relationship to one another.

1

3

4

2

5

8

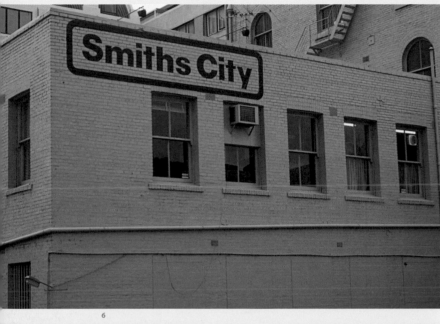

6

7

9

PHOTO 1 *Door bars in Guatemala.* PHOTO 2 *A painting on a building in Mexico.* PHOTO 3 *Vertical half-timbers in a house in Germany. This image influenced* Constructions #32. PHOTO 4 *A beautiful tree in South Africa.* PHOTO 5 *Vertical trunks of trees on our farm.* PHOTO 6 *A building in New Zealand that I loved for the color, the windows, and the shape.* PHOTOS 7 AND 8 *Horizontal slats of a barn wall .* PHOTO 9 *Horizontal gesture of petals on a flower, South Africa.*

***Constructions #74***, ©2003.
46¼" × 57½". 100 percent
cotton fabrics hand-dyed
by Nancy Crow. Fabrics
cut and machine-pieced
improvisationally by
Nancy Crow. Hand-quilted
by Marla Hattabaugh
with pattern denoted by
Nancy Crow.

Mara Hattabaugh hand-quilted Constructions #75 in the
large studio in the Crow Timber Frame Barn.

*Constructions #75*, ©2004.
38½″ × 48½″. 100 percent
cotton fabrics hand-dyed
by Nancy Crow. Fabrics
cut and machine-pieced
improvisationally by
Nancy Crow. Hand-quilted
by Marla Hattabaugh
with pattern denoted by
Nancy Crow.

*Constructions #76*, ©2004.
37¼" × 66". 100 percent
cotton fabrics hand-dyed
by Nancy Crow. Fabrics
cut and machine-pieced
improvisationally by
Nancy Crow. Hand-quilted
by Marla Hattabaugh
with pattern denoted by
Nancy Crow.

*The Crow Timber Frame Barn with my work installed in June 2004.*

*Looking for a Reprieve!,*
©1993–1994. 81½″ × 81″.
100 percent cotton fabrics
hand-dyed by Nancy Crow.
Fabrics cut and machine-
pieced by Nancy Crow.
Hand-quilted by Marie
Moore with pattern
denoted by Nancy Crow.

**Constructions #77: Looking for a Reprieve!**, ©2004. 53" × 89¼". 100 percent cotton fabrics hand-dyed by Nancy Crow. Fabrics cut and machine-pieced improvisationally by Nancy Crow. Hand-quilted by Marla Hattabaugh with pattern denoted by Nancy Crow.

JANUARY 11, 2004 | SKETCHBOOK NOTES

Constructions #77: Looking for a Reprieve! *I hope to finish the sewing on this composition—difficult. It has been so hard to compose, but exhilarating. And I hope liberating, somehow. I have been up and down the step ladder so many times. This has been an extremely* PHYSICAL *quilt. My knees have ached, especially after all day working. I could feel them during the night. . . . They have to hold up for 25 more years of quiltmaking.* CONTINUES NOVEMBER 15, 2004 *Keeping my mind on task. Focused. Disciplined. Looking out the south window of Studio #3, I see layers of figurations on top of layers of figurations on top of layers of figurations, all the way down to the huge timber-frame barn. Why do the linear patterns on top of linear patterns take my attention away from working on my slides? The sun is nearly at midpoint, high in the sky. In* Constructions #77, *I went back and re-examined my earlier quilt, opposite.* Looking for a Reprieve! *is about seeking permission to be free.*

# INTERVIEW WITH NANCY CROW

THE FOLLOWING ARE excerpts from a tape-recorded interview with Nancy Crow. The interview took place in Baltimore, Ohio, on December 18, 2002, and was conducted by Jean Robertson for the Archives of American Art, Smithsonian Institution. Some sentences have been slightly edited to help the flow of the excerpts. The full transcript of the interview can be found on the web site of the Archives of American Art: http://artarchives.si.edu/oralhist/crow02.htm

*by Jean Robertson, Ph.D., Associate Professor of Art History, Indiana University, Herron School of Art and Design (IUPUI), based on an interview conducted for Smithsonian Archives of American Art*

JEAN ROBERTSON: How do you start working on a new series of quilts? Do you always work in series?

NANCY CROW: I have discovered that working in a series is important because there's a tendency on the part of an artist to want to resolve everything in one piece, and I think that's a grand mistake because it's biting off too much. So why not break it down and start at some point and do that piece, see what's wrong with it, go on to the next piece and resolve that problem? At the same time, you're constantly making connections back and forth. As you go on, the whole thing gets richer and richer. Nonetheless, when you see the whole series of, let's say, 20 pieces, maybe number two is still a knockout piece. It could still be one of the best pieces.

But I find in teaching, because quiltmaking is such a slow process, that people have this anxiety about, "Well, I've got to do it all in this one piece because I've given six months, eight months of my life to do it." And I'll say over and over, "No, you don't have to, because you're already biting off more than you can handle." You have to figure out where your ground is—visually, or with color, or with shapes and lines, or with proportions, or with composition—and bring it back to a level where you can make some progress and not drown.

JR: For yourself, what would be the trigger for a series? What usually starts you off?

NC: Well, I honestly have never had real problems coming up with ideas. If anything, I have more ideas than I know how to sift through. For me it's reining myself in and saying, "You've got to get focused, because you're just letting your brain go all over the place, just kind of running around."

Generally an idea, for me, is going to end up being expressed in geometric form. In other words, I'm not interested in doing landscape, although I may have looked out my window at the landscape—like, *Constructions #17* is definitely about tall trees, but it comes out as line, all vertical lines. I don't want it to obviously look like trees. All my newest quilts are under the umbrella of "constructions." That idea hit me in 1995, although I didn't pick up on it again until 1997. I've now made 64 quilts that are all under the umbrella of "things being constructed." That's all I need, for an idea in my mind; it just takes me in so many different directions in how things fit together like puzzles.

JR: Did that relate to moving [the timber frame] barn onto your property at all?

NC: Yes, I think it did, because if you go into the huge main room of the barn and look at the roof, you'll see the ceiling is gridded, the way the wood has been put together.

JR: When you work on a series like—let's take *Constructions*—do you work on one quilt and finish it, and then the second and finish it, or do you work on many at once? Take me through your process.

NC: I am a person who gets bored very easily, so I need to be multitasked and I need to be stimulated all the time, so for me, it's better to work on multiple pieces. It's better to have at least three, if not more, quilts going at the same time so if I get stopped on this one, I can move over to another wall. And since I've taught myself to work this way, I've become far more efficient and happier about doing my artwork and wanting to be in my studio.

JR: How long have you been doing it that way, working on several at once? Did you figure that out pretty early on?

NC: I think this, frankly, came after you interviewed me the last time [in 1988]. By 1990, I had had it with quiltmaking. I was sick of it. I hated it. I said, "This is it. If I don't learn how to work in a new, different way, I'm outta here, because I'm not going to give another bit of my time to making quilts," because it had become so tedious. I was working with templates. All my work was mirror-imaged and symmetrical. I knew that I could never really go on if I didn't figure out a way to get out of this. My work had gotten incredibly complex with prints, but I felt like in some ways I had dug myself into a hole. Nineteen-ninety was a pivotal year. I made virtually nothing that entire year, except for one tiny piece. I kept working on it, thinking, "Why can't I allow myself to work asymmetrically?" I kept trying and I kept trying, and I didn't know how to do it.

I finally made a piece that year that was sort of on its way, but it took me another three years to break through, to work improvisationally.

JR: I think at the time that I interviewed you, you were just starting to look at some African-American quilts.

NC: [It was particularly important] for me to see the work of Anna Williams. I didn't understand how it was going to impact me, but I knew that it shocked me when I saw her work. Anna Williams is about 72 or 73. She lives in Baton Rouge, Louisiana. She's totally self-taught in her quiltmaking. She started making quilts on what I'd call a regular basis when she was 58. She has now made over 300 quilts. When I saw them for the first time, it would have been 1988, '89, and I was dumbstruck because she hadn't used a ruler. And I just thought, What's wrong with me? Why did I think quilts had to be made with a ruler? Why did everything have to be straight? Why did I bite that off, hook, line, and sinker? So, seeing her quilts, the fact that the line actually could be what I call sensuous, or lyrical, just blew me out of the water. At the time, I could see this in passing, but it hadn't really kicked in. It took another couple of years for it to really slap me up around the face. And she never used a ruler. Everything she did was with scissors, so that's why the lines were crooked, because she just cut the way she felt.

JR: Working more intuitively.

NC: Yes, working totally intuitively. That's when the bell went off in me. I knew I wasn't going to start using scissors like Anna, but I thought, "I can take that darn rotary cutter and I can start to use it in a more expressive way." And I did. But it took me two years. I really believe you have to train the muscles. The muscles have to work with your eye and your heart. It all has to be a coordinated effort.

JR: It's like a physical skill.

NC: Yes. To me it's like practicing drawing. The muscles have to get good enough to make that pencil go where you want it to go.

JR: Do you use the cutter as fluidly as if it was a pencil?

NC: Oh, I'm pretty fluid. I would say that when I'm really working, cracking in my studio, I almost can sense it; it takes a couple of days, but once I start to find my footing again, I can feel the rhythm. It just flows through me into the sewing machine, into the cutting board, and back and forth, back and forth. I love it, because that calms me. It's meditative.

JR: So now you don't draw the designs?

NC: I never do. Never. All that work in there is done by eye.

JR: But what about when you used to do the symmetrical ones?

NC: Up to 1990 my compositions were done with templates, and my work was very intellectualized. The only thing that wasn't intellectualized was what went into the shape. In other words, I pre-cut and made all my shapes and they all fit together like a puzzle, but what went inside those is the part that was intuitive, and that's what I loved about quiltmaking. But I didn't understand how to take it outside those parameters, and that's what I learned in the early 1990s. I honestly think, frankly, what I taught myself during that time and learned and then went out and taught on some level has been the big turning point in contemporary quiltmaking. People who have studied with me understand that, but anybody who's outside of it would not understand because they don't know how I teach. I came up with ways to cut shapes and directly piece them without any templates, with nothing.

But again, to emphasize this: I have never taught anything about the core way I work to anybody and I never will. When I die, it's gone, because that's who I am. It has taken years and years of working so hard to understand how to do these things technically, and I guess I feel like that's not information that any artist ever really in the end gives out. I mean, that is who they are and that's what their work is. I don't know, maybe I'm wrong, but I don't want to, I'm not prepared to, because it's how I can make things happen, like in *Constructions # 41*. It's been so hard to get to that point.

JR: Yes. I wonder if people could even physically do it, if what you're saying is correct that you have to kinesthetically learn how.

NC: It has a lot to do with the eye. You know, we were talking about what's important. I would say what I really love are proportions. When I see proportions that are on target, I just feel overwhelmed. So it's proportions as much as anything.

JR: Of one shape to the next?

NC: Of a line to a line, a line to a shape, how they all fit together and work in a composition. And I just go crazy over that.

JR: Do you still use as many colors?

NC: In a given piece? I would say no. I probably have pared that back to some degree, but it doesn't mean I might not in the future. I find personally that being more and more spare is the hardest, because the proportions have to be right on. And to me, it's all instinctive. It's all by eye. You have to keep re-cutting. I'm willing to just cut and cut and throw away and throw away to make it happen, which I guess would be the same thing as erasing or painting over.

JR: What do you think when you look back at the earlier, symmetrical series?

NC: I almost don't know who that person was. I really don't. I feel sometimes like I don't know who the person was anymore.

JR: When did you make the break from working with patterned fabrics?

NC: I would say that 1989 was the last year I worked in my old, traditional way with commercial prints. Starting in 1990, I started little by little working with hand-dyed solids. I actually tried this year to work with prints again, and I can't do it. It's a whole different way of thinking. In many ways I have a lot of respect for my early work because it's one thing to cut parts out as shapes made of colors; it's another thing to think of shapes filled up with visual texture.

JR: What attracts you to solids now?

NC: I think it's because I'm so in love with pure shape and line and proportions, and I feel like I need to get those so tight and so squared away under my belt, and I still think I have a lot of work to do with that. I mean, I think one is always teaching oneself, fine-tuning one's eye visually.

JR: Can you describe your studio routine? Do you work every day?

NC: Well, I think as an artist, first of all you have to be very driven to develop. I don't know where the drive comes from. And then the next thing is you have to figure out how to focus your thoughts and your energies so you're productive. And I think that one of the big struggles for an artist is always the administrative side versus the artistic side. I would be the first to say that an ongoing struggle for me is how to balance out the administrative side so that it doesn't eat up week after week after week. I find that when I become committed to doing my artwork, all of a sudden the administrative work becomes so unimportant to me that I let a lot of stuff go that needs to be attended to. I find that I'm good about getting into my studio at a set time and I'm a workaholic. If I get into the routine of being down at my huge studio in the timber-frame barn—particularly down there—let's say, by no later than 8:30 A.M., I will go up for meals, but I'll often work till 10 or 11 at night, day after day. And I physically can do it. I have a lot of stamina and I love doing it.

JR: And when you're in your studio, are you in silence, or do you play music?

NC: I play music, but I realize that it's just noise, because I have a very vivid imagination. I'm pretty much inside my brain. I do like to try to make connections—I don't know how to put it a better way—these are connections that I think only come when you're relaxed. In other words, I try to let myself go deeper into my work.

Actually, that's where I am in my work now. I'm trying to work up to a much higher level. And it also means I have no one to talk to, because almost nobody in quiltmaking is trying to do that anymore. Most people plateau and they stay at their plateau, but I'm trying to make inroads into understanding where I can go with the work. And part of that is by doing the work, seeing results, analyzing the results, and part is just simply saying, "You know, you can do better than this."

JR: So you set a really high bar for yourself.

NC: Yes. That's the way I am. And I'm, frankly, pretty disappointed that almost nobody in quiltmaking is willing to do that. I'm going to just say it for the record. I feel very strongly about it. One of the disappointing things for me is that most people sell out their talent. I don't know why. I think it takes enormous courage and enormous character to keep on with your work knowing full well that at any point in time, the work may not be acceptable to anybody but yourself.

One thing I realize now at my age is that you have to work incredibly hard. You really have to work hard. You have to be so critical of what you're doing, just to know what's procrastination and what's repetitive and what's junk, and weed it out of your work and get on.

JR: You have an absolutely incredible studio here, this former barn. What do you want your work space to do for you?

NC: Well, I want that big, open space like I have now, with lots and lots of pin walls because I hate the inefficiency of taking something down. If you only have one wall to work on, then you're going to have to take the current piece down in order to work on the next thing, and that is just totally backwards. I always say I like to go from A to B very quickly; I can't stand going backwards. So I believe if you have talent, then you do everything you can to support the talent and encourage the talent. That includes having all those white pin walls, having color-corrected lighting, having multiple tables.

After having my knees replaced, it took me eight years before I could go up and down a ladder again. And now that my legs are strong enough and I can do it, I can work on big pieces. I'd never be able to do them in that space at the house because visually I can never get far enough away from them. I'm working on really large line and shapes, and you've got to have a distance to see what they're doing. They almost look awkward up close. It's been a gift to have all this space and it's been a challenge because it's made me start to re-examine composition on a much larger scale, which I want to do, but then I also like going back to work on a really intimate scale up at the smaller studio.

JR: Do you think handwork is a dying direction in quiltmaking?

NC: This is another sad thing. I am a piecer. Piecing means I put one fabric together with another fabric, either by hand with a running stitch or I do it with a machine. I happen to be a machine-piecer. Well, the way our whole culture is going now, machine-piecing is going to be a lost art also because it is too time-consuming. The way many quilts are being made today is by the use of what is called Wonder Under, which is basically a soluble glue that goes on the back of fabrics. And that is how quilts are being made because it is fast. It's very sad. I think in another 50 years, a machine-pieced quilt is going to be considered valuable just because of the amount of technical work in it.

JR: I know that some of your series in the past had specific content. You worked on a series when your mother died, the *Passion* series [1983 to 1985]. You worked on the *Bittersweet* series [1980 to 1982] that I remember you saying was about the relationship between a man and a woman. Do you still feel like autobiography and your personal experiences are something you're thinking about in your quilts?

NC: I would say that when that happens, it happens naturally. I don't go looking for an emotional content. It isn't necessarily happening now, except that I am trying to do more authentic work for myself. So if there's any emotion involved, that's it.

I don't know if you're familiar with the *Chinese Souls* quilts that I did after I came back from China. The Ohio Arts Council did an exchange with China, and four of us were chosen to go. It was in September 1990, which was the year after Tiananmen Square. Susan Shie and I were doing a little sightseeing with an interpreter. We came out of the Blue Goose Pagoda and heard sirens coming from police cars. All of a sudden, right up in front of us—because we had come out and we were standing right there on the edge of the street— police cars came up near us and right behind them was a huge truck—like a cattle truck with wooden sides. Standing in the cattle truck were young men packed like sardines. They were about the age of my kids at the time, in their teens and early 20s.

The next thing I noticed was that every single one of these young men and boys was tied with heavy rope. It wound around their necks or heads some way, around their shoulders, and their heads were pulled over, with their hands bound behind their backs. And finally I asked the interpreter, "What is going on?" and she wouldn't tell us. So I said, "You're going to have to tell me what's going on," because by that time another cattle truck had pulled up. They were stopped there in front of us because the traffic was so dense, and all these sirens were blaring on and on. And finally the interpreter, in a very hesitant emotional voice, told me that they were being driven around the city as a deterrent to scare people because they were on their way to being executed.

I said to the interpreter, "What have they done?" She was so upset, that's why she didn't want to tell me. What they had done were absolutely the most nothing things, like pick pocketing. Absolutely minor things. But she said, "They don't care because there are so many people and they want to stop crime, so they just drive these men around to scare people because they know they are going to be executed."

Well, unbeknownst to Susan and me, the painter and sculptor, who came to China with us, were stationed at the Xi'an Academy of Art. The school was located right across from where these boys were being taken. When we got back together a couple of days later where we stayed in the same compound, they told us, "You know, it's the strangest thing, but there's a huge, long, white wall across from the Art Academy. They came out and they were painting all these black dots and they put all this calligraphy under the dots. And we asked what was going on, and they said they had just executed a lot of young men and that they had to put the writing on the wall so parents could come and find out what had happened to their children."

Well, I had a piece of fabric with me; what is called a fat quarter, and it had been resist-dyed, with 16 circles. And I had some hand-embroidery thread and I started embroidering around each of these circles. And then I made a grid.

JR: A grid?

NC: I made a grid, but this grid had meaning. It went through the circles, because they told us that each of those boys had to kneel down on the ground. They put the gun up and shot them right at the base of the neck. So basically, the cross—you die on the cross, or whatever, and you're killed, right there. And this is the rope going around them. So I called them *Chinese Souls*. I made ten quilts in rapid succession when I got home.

JR: It looks like the crosshairs of a gun, too.

NC: Yes, the crosshairs of a gun, too. All of that. I was like a maniac there in China until I had that little thing embroidered. And that's the only thing that saved me before we got out of that country, because we were about halfway through the month by then. So that series of quilts was very, very emotional for me and it had a reason for being. But that happens only if it happens. I don't go looking for a subject to happen.

JR: At other times have you had a political or sociological message in your quilts?

NC: No. I really think my work is about beauty, frankly. That's what I want, beauty in what you see. And really, I want you to go into a gallery or museum and see this hanging and react to it just on that level without knowing if there is any meaning behind it.

JR: What about your travels as an influence on your work? You were in China and this specific event happened. I know you've been to Mexico.

NC: South Africa has had a big influence, I think. But it all comes out more in the graphic and the improvisational approach to creating the object. It's not so much the social dynamics or the politics or the poverty or those kinds of things I would find in those countries.

JR: So it's not really a narrative or a story about the country.

NC: No.

JR: It's more the colors or textures or patterns that you create?

NC: Right. Right. Particularly with my collections [of textiles and objects from around the world], it's just constantly looking for patterning. I think that's what I'm looking for, patterning; and what is the patterning doing; and why is it doing what it's doing? Just always looking for relationships.

JR: And when you collect something, you're making a pattern, in a way, by displaying a dozen wooden fish next to each other.

NC: Yes. I love that. I just have to see things in rows and congregated. It makes me feel really happy.

JR: Besides working on pattern and shape and composition, are there technical problems? I know you've done a lot of innovations with strip-piecing. Are some quilts, some series just simply because you're trying to work out some technical issue?

NC: It's not even a technical issue as much as what I've discovered. By sticking with a process—(I'm just going to use the process here of strip-piecing, which is a way of working technically)—by working with it over and over, year after year, doors have opened and I have discovered ways of working that no one has ever used before. Not that I'm looking for ways that no one else has worked before. But I have opened doors to ways of creating a more expressive composition just because I've understood technically how to do it with strip-piecing. And it wouldn't have happened if I hadn't practiced strip-piecing all these years. There's no way, because none of what I'm doing is written up anywhere, so I couldn't have learned it from someone else.

JR: So you've got a technical mastery that comes from experience.

NC: Absolutely. And I believe that is part of the hard work of being an artist, particularly an artist who's doing what I would consider fresh work.

JR: Does the function of quilts ever play a part in the meaning of your work?

NC: No. I never think about it. In fact I think sometimes, why do I make quilts, since quilts are so looked down upon in the art world? I've been talking about it with a friend of mine who loves to piece as much as I do, and we both came to the conclusion there's just no way to explain it to anyone else. You're just absolutely consumed. I'm consumed by machine-piecing. I'm consumed by cutting up fabric and putting pieces back together. And I don't know why. It's when I really feel happy.

JR: Besides individual pieces within a series, do you think certain series are more significant?

NC: Hmm. I don't necessarily think that way. I guess what I would say is some series are small just in and of their nature, like the *Passion* series I did about my mother when she was dying. That was it. That was all I had to say about it at the time. Whereas the *Constructions* series keeps growing. One of the comments made to me by a man in Philadelphia in October [2002] at my exhibition, which contained the biggest number of the *Constructions* series quilts at one showing was, "Do you realize that within this group of 22 quilts, you have enough ideas to work off the rest of your life?" I have a hard time being totally linear; my mind's always going so fast. I tend to think, okay, if my mind wants to go over there, I'll go over there. So I probably have about eight different themes under the *Constructions* umbrella, any one of which I could go and run with and it too would probably start sprouting laterals. My mind or brain is always crowded with ideas.

So within this particular series right now, I have tons of ideas I've jotted down in my sketchbooks that come up as I'm working, I have to just get the fleeting idea down before it's lost. I would say the *Constructions* series and the *Color Blocks* series are the two series for which I've had tons of ideas. But *Color Blocks* I'm done with. I have no more interest in that.

JR: Is it just recently that you've been dyeing fabrics? How did that all come about?

NC: I have to go all the way back to when I was a weaver in the 1970s, actually even back to the late 1960s, in graduate school, where dyeing our yarns was a very important part of our education. For some reason I never transferred to quiltmaking the idea that I could dye my own fabrics. It actually came about by watching other groundbreakers—namely Jan Myers-Newberry. I didn't start dyeing probably until 1991. So I was really late to it.

JR: Before that, you were using store bought fabrics?

NC: Pretty much commercial fabrics except for the occasional hand-dyed I bought from someone else. What happens when one starts hand-dyeing is that one's fabrics become very unique. Our fabrics look different because there is what we call a "hand" to how you dye the fabric and it takes on a personality and a characteristic that's you. So, after a while, I couldn't use other people's hand-dyed fabrics. They had to be mine. It would be the same for a painter mixing paint, I would mix my colors my own certain way. I would assume that's what a painter does. He doesn't have someone else mixing his colors for him.

JR: Your colors look very saturated.

NC: The way I dye is like a watercolorist. I dye one layer of color, process it, then I re-dye the fabric, process it, and I do it a third time, and so the color has a very saturated depth, which I like. That's the only way I can get it, by triple-dyeing.

JR: I know you have huge quantities in your studio.

NC: Yes. I still don't have the kind of sophistication I'd really like, which includes just the slightest stepping down. I would like a huge range of "cold and warm" or "flat and luminous" colors, thousands. I'd like to have that kind of range, but I don't have it because I haven't dyed it, basically.

JR: Do you always use the same kind of fabric, or do you dye on different fabrics?

NC: No, I'm pretty much consistent now. I use a type of cotton broadcloth. It's a very good-quality fabric. It's fairly hard to hand-quilt when the interstices of the cotton structure get filled with dye. According to my hand-quilter, it gets harder and harder to get the needle through because the dye actually fills up the interstices in the weaving.

JR: The other thing you mentioned was your sketchbooks. I wanted to ask you about what role keeping the sketchbooks has had.

NC: I'm pretty diligent now about keeping a running commentary and a running group of photographs about works in progress as I'm doing them and the sequence in which my work is made. I didn't do such a good job prior to 1990, but I've been pretty good about it since 1990. I need to spend more time going back through my notebooks because I feel like I've got so many good ideas that I jotted in there and then I let go of them and never go back to them again because I'm on to something else.

I also keep anything written that will psychologically propel me forward. I tend to keep those kinds of things, like quotes. This [sketchbook includes an article about] one of the artists I admire probably more than anybody else, and that's Rosalie Gascoigne, who grew up in New Zealand but moved to Australia as a young wife. She is actually considered an Australian artist. She was a sculptor. What I like about her is that she is absolutely, ruthlessly honest in her reflections about herself and her work. And I like that. I like people to be straightforward. One of the things she said that to me is extremely important: "You can choose to go deep or you can choose to go wide." And then she said, "I chose to go deep in my career." And it really made me think. It helped me to hear her say, "Wow! My studio is too small! If I could have my druthers, I would want a whole airplane hangar."

JR: So much of your work you have to do by yourself. In fact, you said you didn't like to have an assistant. You have Marla [Hattabaugh] doing the quilting, but otherwise you like to work alone. Do you ever start to feel isolated?

NC: No. I like it. I love it. Maybe that's why I teach, because it does get me out. Maybe one of the reasons I've been able to be successful to some degree, is I love being by myself. I happen to believe that the more solitude you have, the more you're able to delve inside and find those rich levels of ability that are fresh. Otherwise you're allowing all this chattering constantly coming at you and you can never reach into that part of yourself, whatever that part is. It takes a kind of calming down to let yourself reach in there. I know a lot of people who will tell me, "I could never live out on a farm like you do; I could never live the way you live," who are artists. They need a city, they need traffic, they need people to meet.

JR: How about the goals that you still want to realize in your art, in your work. Do you have definable goals?

NC: You know, I don't know where I can go with my work in terms of personal development. All I know or feel is that I want to keep growing and changing. I want the growth and change to be, in a sense, organic. I want it to be because it's feeding on what I've learned beforehand.

# DEDICATION

In terms of making my way through life, I like to think I have an enormous reservoir of emotional strength that helps me make the journey all by myself. But that is a conceit I have never had to test or experience because for the past 40 years I have been surrounded by a small and loyal band of three men—my husband John and our sons Nathaniel and Matthew.

I married John Stitzlein in 1965 when I was 22 and he was 23, and he told me he could take a bride to live in Quito, Ecuador, the focus country of his master's degree research in agricultural economics. Although employed by Ohio State University, John was planning to work on a project for USAID, the United States Agency for International Development. I wanted to travel and I wanted adventure—and so did John.

John and I had known each other since our mid teens, when we became square-dancing partners. Over five years of dating, I learned how mature he was for his age. Centered, disciplined, and a conscientious worker, he was also innately thoughtful, generous, and partial to helping others. Within months of our first date, he took on handyman chores and seasonal maintenance for my widowed mother. In the fall of each year, he would volunteer to remove the heavy window and door screens from her aging house—downstairs and up—then in spring he would wash them and put them back. When I was in undergraduate and graduate school, John helped me unfailingly with loading and firing kilns in the ceramics lab. When I took up weaving he helped warp looms, and later he sometimes helped mark quilt tops. Without exception, John has supported my love of ceramics, textiles, art, and collecting. An adventurer, he studied in Mexico City in his junior year of college; he lived in Venezuela as an exchange student during his senior year; and he hoped to live and work overseas after graduate school. John always loved being outdoors but was never a hunter; over the years, he has evolved into a conservationist, sensitive to all of life's struggles.

It was John's longing to live on a farm that led to our purchasing land in 1979, giving me the "privilege" of experiencing space and privacy and the life opportunity to understand what solitude can mean. When I needed to

expand my work spaces, John rose to the challenge of finding, saving, and renovating three timber-frame barns that we transformed into studios. He did all this while holding a stressful and time-consuming position at Ohio State University. With a farmer's physical strength, John tackled his fourth and largest renovation soon after his retirement from the University.

John is the most nonjudgmental person I have ever met, a very great attribute when coupled with the intensely emotional seesaws of being married to an artist. Because he has always had an exceptional sense of who he is, one of John's most valuable gifts to me has been his ability to teach me how to stay centered. When our sons were young, he urged me to take time to go to my studio and work. He encouraged me not to give up and never to feel guilty about time not used elsewhere. When my teaching career began, he took charge of the boys and insisted that I accept offers to teach in Germany or Australia or South Africa, emphasizing that such opportunities may not come again. Most of all, John always encouraged me to accept the responsibility and sacrifices that decidedly come with having talent.

With great admiration, I also dedicate this book to our two sons, Nathaniel John Stitzlein and Matthew Crow Stitzlein, who have contributed so much to the creative life we lead on our farm. Over 22 years, Nathaniel and Matthew helped with the planting of thousands of hardwood and flowering tree seedlings and subsequent transplantings. They took part in many of the house and all of the barn renovations. They took the lead, along with my husband, in the grand makeover of a huge Poling family barn into a large studio and teaching facility that is now The Crow Timber Frame Barn. Matthew led the charge with his exceptional engineering skills, his sense of spatial relation-

ABOVE Nancy Crow and John Stitzlein in Ecuador, fall 1995, selecting embroidery for blouses.

ships, his love of beautiful proportions, and his attention to detail. Nathaniel is my partner in the Barn Workshops and helps lead the international tours we conduct. He is the talented designer behind my web site. Nathaniel married and brought into our family Michelle Salrin Stitzlein, an artist/sculptor whose medium is the restructuring of found and recycled objects. It is a rare gift to have a daughter-in-law with whom I can have serious conversations about art and exchange ideas, hopes, and frustrations. My sons and daughter-in-law are wise, insightful, honest and loyal participants in a shared and ongoing love of the creative life.

Today, John and I continue to live on the farm we both intensely love, surrounded by our wonderful varieties of hardwood and flowering trees. We watch as they change with the seasons, becoming more stately with each passing year. We watch while they provide homes for nesting birds, and we sometimes watch while they wither and die. John and I each have a large studio to work in . . . he, with his massive collection of machine parts, bolts, engines, and farm machinery, welding scraps of metal into odd arrangements, bending wire into mobile drawings . . . I twirling through my endless stacks of hand-dyed fabrics, their colors overwhelming my senses, beckoning me all at once, exploding into my vision.

With heartfelt gratitude and love, I dedicate this book to you, John, Nathaniel, and Matthew.

# ACKNOWLEDGMENTS

I WISH TO EXPRESS my profound gratitude to Jean Robertson, Ph.D., Associate Professor of Art History, Herron School of Art and Design, Indiana University, IUPUI, for conducting intelligent and thoughtful interviews with me in my private studios in both 1988 and 2003. These interviews, which are thorough and insightful documents, have been preserved in the Archives of American Art, The Smithsonian Institution, Washington, D.C. Jean has remained a steady supporter of my work and way of life. Wondrously, for this book, she has skillfully distilled an enormous amount of interview material into an articulate foreword that vividly captures my energy and vision, making me very proud and appreciative.

Likewise I am indebted to the loyalty and professionalism of my exceptional photographer, J. Kevin Fitzsimons. He has documented my finished work, works-in-progress, and studio walls since 1987. With great patience, calm, and total perfectionism, he has built a photographic legacy that has made this book possible.

I have been fortunate in finding first-rate hand-quilters in every decade of my career. These are women whose fine stitching has satisfied my own perfectionist demands. Since 1988, after introducing herself to me and asking if I would consider hiring her to hand-quilt my work, Marla Hattabaugh has taken one quilt top after the other and stitched the closely marked lines to my specifications. Likewise, over many years, Marie Moore and Kris Doyle beautifully and expertly hand-quilted many tops from several series of work: *Double Mexican Wedding Rings, Bow Tie, Chinese Souls, Linear Studies,* and *Color Blocks.* Other fine hand-quilters I want to thank include Elizabeth Miller, Brenda Stultz, Lou DeLay, Sue Milling, Gail Chatterson, Mary Underwood, and Mildred Minchey. Anna Mae Gazo has been my only machine-quilter. I am forever indebted to all of you for your beautiful workmanship.

I want to acknowledge Mike Shreyer, my long-time carpenter, who helped create the beautiful spaces in both my home and studios from 1980 to 1995.

I also wish to thank Marty Bowne, Ginie Curtze, and Susan Seagram, for acknowledging and encouraging my teaching skills by providing arenas in the United States, Germany, and France where I have taught some of the most gifted quiltmakers worldwide.

I wish to acknowledge Penny McMorris for her support, through spoken words and essays, and through inclusion of my work in important exhibitions earlier in my career.

Thank you Eichi Hosomi for painting for ten years the fabric ideas I designed. Thank you Anne Knudsen for embracing this huge book project over the last two years. Thank you Kim Bartko for doing such a terrific job designing the book.

And last, I want to thank my extended family for being such an interesting bunch of highly opininated, loving, and supportive people.

# IN MEMORIAM

**RACHEL CROW CAMPOCHIARO 1921 to 2005**

In memory of my sister, nicknamed Betty, whom I adored and admired for her generosity, first-rate eye, perfectionism, and friendship.

**JOSEPH BRUNO SLOWINSKI 1962 to 2001**

In memory of my greatly missed nephew, Dr. Joseph B. Slowinski, renowned expert on venomous snakes, who died in a remote area of Myanmar (Burma) on September 12, 2001, while leading a research expedition for San Francisco's California Academy of Sciences. Joe was beloved by his family, friends, and colleagues, and his loss is still fresh in the hearts and minds of all who knew him. He brightened our lives with his open-minded generosity and his contagious enthusiasm for every kind of adventure and discovery, from finding a new species of spitting cobra to trying out a new recipe for a family reunion.

# SUBJECT INDEX

Detail, *Color Blocks #33*. See full quilt on page 111.

# INDEX OF QUILTS BY NANCY CROW

When two or more quilts are presented on one page, on facing pages, or on gatefold pages, each is presented at a size that reflects its proportion relative to the size of other quilts in the group. **Bold** indicates photographs of full quilts; *italics* indicates photographs of quilt details

# BIOGRAPHY

## OCCUPATION
Artist

## MEDIUM
Quiltmaking

## EDUCATION
Bachelor (1965) and Master (1969) of Fine Arts in Ceramics and Weaving from Ohio State University

## PUBLISHED BOOKS
*Nancy Crow: Improvisational Quilts*. Lafayette, CA: C&T Publishing, 1995

*Gradations: From the Studio of Nancy Crow*. Saddlebrook, NJ: Quilt House Publishing, 1995

*Nancy Crow: Work in Transition*, Peducah, KY: American Quilters' Society, 1992

*Nancy Crow: Quilts and Influences*, Peducah, KY: American Quilters' Society, 1990

## FABRIC DESIGN
*Nancy Crow for Kent Avery*, produced by Westwood, Inc., New York, NY

## EXCHANGE ARTIST
Mainland China, Shaanxi Province, sponsored by The Ohio Arts Council, 1990

## QUILT VENUE ORIGINATION
Quilt National
Quilt/Surface Design Symposium
Art Quilt Network

## AWARDS
1999: Named a Fellow of the American Craft Council, New York, NY

1997: Inducted into the Quilters Hall of Fame, Marion, IN

1996: National Living Treasure Award, University of North Carolina at Wilmington

## GRANTS
2002, 1996, 1988, 1985, 1982, and 1980: Individual Artist's Fellowships from The Ohio Arts Council

1990–1991: Major Fellowship from The Ohio Arts Council

1980: Craftsmen's Fellowship from The National Endowment for the Arts

## MUSEUM COLLECTIONS
The Renwick Gallery, The Smithsonian Institution, Washington, D.C.

The Museum of Arts & Design, New York, NY

The Museum of American Folk Art, New York, NY

Miami University Art Museum, Oxford, OH

Indianapolis Museum of Art, Indianapolis, IN

## RECENT EXHIBITIONS

### 2005
*The Textural Revolution: Early & Recent Works by Dorothy Gill Barnes and Nancy Crow*, Johnson Humrickhouse Museum, Coshocton, OH

*Nancy Crow: Constructions—Color & Spatial Relationships*, Auckland Museum, Auckland, New Zealand

*High Fiber: Objects from the Renwick's Permanent Collection*, Renwick Gallery of the Smithsonian American Art Museum, Washington, D.C.

*Art Quilt Art*, The Quiltfestival Höri 2005, Lake Constance, Germany

*Magnificent Extravagance: Artists & Opulence, Racine Art Museum*, Racine, WI

*Nancy Crow: Constructions—Color & Spatial Relationships*, Hawke's Bay Exhibition Centre, Hastings, New Zealand

*Of Time and Place: Contemporary Layered and Stitched Textiles*, Houston Center for Contemporary Craft, Houston, TX

## 2004

*280/Parameters*, Huntington Museum of Art, Huntington, WV

*The Quilted Surface*, Indiana University Southeast, New Albany, IN

*Fourth Biennial Fiber Survey Exhibition*, Snyderman/Works Galleries, Philadelphia, PA

*Textilekunst und Quilts*, Hermann Hesse Museum & Höri Art Gallery, Lake Constance, Germany

*Artist as Quiltmaker*, Oberlin, OH

*Art-Quilt-Art*, Indiana University of Pennsylvania

*The Textural Revolution: Early & Recent Works by Dorothy Gill Barnes and Nancy Crow*, Johnson Humrickhouse Museum, Coshocton, OH

*Constructions—Color & Spatial Relationships, Nancy Crow Retrospective*, Auckland Museum, Auckland, New Zealand

## 2003

*Invitational Exhibit*, The Richard M. Ross Art Museum, Ohio Wesleyan University

*Fiber Art Today: An Encore Presentation*, Mobilia Gallery, Cambridge, MA

*Fabric Constructions*, Leedy-Voulkos Art Center, Kansas City, MS

*Ohio Pioneers of the Art Quilt*, Snowden Gallery, Ohio State University

*280/Parameters,* Huntington Museum of Art, Huntington, WV

*Cheongju International Craft Biennale*, Cheongju, Korea

## 2002

*30 Distinguished Quiltmakers of the World,* Tokyo Dome Stadium, Tokyo, Japan

*Textiles Two Thousand Two,* Center for Creative Studies, Detroit, MI

*SOFA*, New York, NY

*Eloquent Threads: The Daphne Farago Fiber Art Collection*, Museum of Fine Arts, Boston, MA

*Mary Barringer and Nancy Crow*, Snyderman/Works Gallery, Philadelphia, PA

## 2001

*Ground Cover: Contemporary Quilts* McIlroy Gallery, Niceville, FL

*Crow Timber Frame Barn*, Baltimore, OH

*Quilt National*, Athens, OH

*Quilt Berlin Symposium,* Berlin, Germany

*Solo,* Elzay Gallery, Ada, OH

*Celebrating Contemporary Crafts, 2001*, Providence Art Club, Providence, RI

*SOFA*, Chicago, IL

*New Forms in Fiber: Trends and Traditions*, Mobilia Gallery, Cambridge, MA

## 2000

*Surface-Strength-Structure*, Snyderman/Works Gallery, Philadelphia, PA

*Nancy Crow: Quilts in Depth*, Strasbourg, France

*Small Works*, The Gallery at Studio B, Lancaster, OH

*Eclectic Energy*, The Gallery at Studio B, Lancaster, OH

*Visual Rhythms*, Thirteen Moons Gallery, Santa Fe, NM